INDISPENSABLE BAD DEBT

The Theory of Economic System Gap
and
Credit Cycle

By

Hema Senanayake

authorHOUSE®

AuthorHouse™
1663 Liberty Drive, Suite 200
Bloomington, IN 47403
www.authorhouse.com
Phone: 1-800-839-8640

First published by AuthorHouse   11/12/2008

ISBN: 978-1-4389-3456-3 (sc)
ISBN: 978-1-4389-3457-0 (hc)

Library of Congress Control Number: 2008910720

Printed in the United States of America
Bloomington, Indiana

This book is printed on acid-free paper.

CONTENTS

ACKNOWLEDGMENTS

This book is not possible without the support and inspiration of numerous people. I must admit that I was mostly benefited from those who mercilessly challenged my initial presentations. Therefore, I specially extend my gratitude to Mr. Ajith Collonne, Dr. Krassimir Petrove, and Professor Kumar David.

Mr. Robert G. Britt, the president of Quantum Tubers Corporation, always boosts my morale when I share a thought with him. I extend my gratitude to him for those kind words and suggestions.

I am not sure why my father, Sampson, at the age of ninety and my mother, Ghana (eighty-four), are still fascinated by seeing me involved in literary work. My father-in-law, Hurbet Mendis, is also interested in my literary work, and he even read the initial draft and made some corrections. Those seniors always have a string of inspiration on the younger generation. I owe them.

My final expression of gratitude goes to my wife Sheeva and my daughter Dinushi Vidyanga, who patiently tolerated my intermittent, long periods of absence from home for five years as a result of my research work.

PREFACE

"Even bad debt is good credit," said U.S. President Herbert Hoover. Some economists lament that the modern economies are extremely "debt based." According to some estimates, current global output is $50 trillion, while implicit debt amounts to over $300 trillion.

It would be more appropriate if we characterized the economy as based on "bad debt" not only because these cumulative debts can never be paid, but also because most of the debt will have to be written off from time to time as we practice economy today. There is no escape from this fate.

The recessions and financial crises that occurred in 1929, 1970, and 2007 are significantly different from the economic recessions that occurred in between these crises. These particular years denote the approximate years of the beginning of what I call "terminal recessions," during which a massive amount of debt would have to be canceled.

I used the word "terminal" only to intimate that the economy cannot remain as it is or grow any more even if the physical potential exists without the cancellation of a good part of debt, especially consumer debt.

While writing off of debt from the account books is likely to be related to the circumstances of individual cases, a more general cancellation of debt should also occur through a process of moderate inflation and corresponding wage adjustment.

Any attempt by the financial authorities to stop this general debt cancellation process during a terminal recession by preventing moderate inflation and discouraging wage adjustments could aggravate and prolong the crisis.

These phenomena are explained through a new economic theory that I have called the "theory of economic system gap and credit cycle."

The economic system gap is simply defined as the gap between consumer income (which is less) and the value of consumption in any given accounting period.

The relative success of western capitalism should be attributed to the introduction of mechanisms to bridge this gap knowingly or unknowingly. In periods of economic progress, the gap was bridged, while, in periods of terminal recessions, this bridging mechanism failed.

Similarly, the relative economic failure of Soviet- or Cuban-style "socialism" is attributed to their inability to create a sustainable "gap" and bridge it on a continuous basis, rather than the political structure of these societies. It is self-evident that such a process is possible only in an enterprise-based economy irrespective of the ownership of enterprises.

In addition, economic failure in most developing countries where a basic capitalist infrastructure exists is nothing but the failure to create a sustainable "economic system gap" and develop a satisfactory bridging mechanism. Again, these hypotheses are explained through the theory of economic system gap and credit cycle.

Therefore, the importance of the theory explained in this book does not need to be exaggerated.

This book is about the theory of economic system gap and credit cycle. Economic theory books are usually addressed to fellow economists, and making them intelligible to other lay intellectuals is considered secondary.

Yet, this book is addressed to the general public, whom I believe need to understand matters of economics to influence the economic policy of the country. If they do so, our democracy would become more meaningful.

I have a long-held belief that the right to make economic policy is an inalienable right of the citizenry. To exercise this right, people need to attain a certain knowledge level. I hope that this book contributes to bridging this knowledge gap too.

A Note to the Reader

Several CEOs in Wall Street who were considered as the finest people in America have now become the worst of the kind at this moment of writing in September 2008.

If the current financial crisis is explained as something related to the extreme greediness of the CEOs of financial institutions (although there can be a small element of it), then we are sure to ignore the real cause, and, as a result, we will miss the opportunity to formulate the real solution too.

This is a system crisis that needs to be resolved proactively. I clearly visualized what was to come ahead as far back as May 2007 through the theory explained in this book. At that time, the stock market in the United States was in good swing. The rate of employment was high, and the growth of the economy was good.

However, analyzing the issue of debt through the said economic theory I wrote on May 8, 2007, to Ajith Collonne, a university teacher, and said "As this debt nationally and internationally can never be paid, credit cycle would eventually bring negative pressure on consumers and as a result on production too. Then it is required to abandon the old credit cycle and start a new one. Or else it will adjust by itself through violent disruption of production and through economic depression. Human kind would prefer the first option and hence the year of debt cancellation within nation states and globally would come sooner than later."

As predicted, the time has now come to abandon the old credit cycle, as this book went to press in September 2008.

I knew that it was quite difficult for economists to imagine a situation where part of the debt is canceled in general. However, this has happened several times in the past, and it is going to happen in this moment of history. If we do not proactively cancel part of the debt through an acceptable mechanism, still debt will be cancelled out by disruption of production through a recession. Cancellation of debt, especially consumer debt, is an economic necessity that I will explain in this book.

The U.S. government's recent decision to absorb bad debt of financial institutions and transfer them to the tax-paying consumers is not a solution.

If the government move is to absorb bad debt in order to cancel it in the future, then it could be regarded as a tactical decision, since it might help to stop the total collapse of the financial mechanism on which production itself is rested upon.

To understand this whole issue, we need to understand a little bit of economic theory.

In the contemporary economic system, the aggregate consumer income is always less than the aggregate value of consumption. The value of consumption is not the total output; instead, it is what the producer entrepreneurs expect from consumers out of their expenditure from the act of consumption. If entrepreneurs did not get back what they expected from consumers, then they cannot continue production.

Therefore, at least consumer expenditure should be equal to the value of consumption in order to put the economic system into equilibrium. So, how do consumers, as a collective group of people, spend a sum of money equal to the value of consumption? The short answer is consumer credit. In fact, it is the consumer credit mechanism that mainly puts the economic system into equilibrium, which ensures that entrepreneurs get back what they expect.

If the gap between consumer income and the value of consumption is defined as the economic system gap, then we can summarize what began to happen in August 2007 in the United States as follows.

During periods of economic growth the economic system gap is bridged while during major recessions the bridging mechanism failed. Knowingly or unknowingly the economic system gap is primarily set to be bridged by consumer credit. Therefore any failure of consumer credit mechanism should trigger a major recession. That is what began to happen in late 2007 in the United States. All other economic ills are just ramifications, not the cause.

When the European fund providers decided to pull the plug on the supply of funds to the subprime housing market in August 2007, the stage was set for the failure of the credit mechanism and, in turn, the failure of bridging the economic system gap.

Then, investors over reacted to the news, creating a financial turmoil. As a result, the credit crunch was aggravated, thereby deeply disturbing the bridging mechanism of the system gap. So, recession was imminent.

The Federal Reserve Board reduced interest rates. However, enough credit did not flow into the economy. The government provided a $170 billion stimulus package, but the bridging mechanism continued to fail.

Then, in September 2008, the U.S. Department of Treasury decided to absorb massive amounts of bad debt of financial institutions. After hearing this news, the stock market bounced back. Most of the reports suggested quickly that perhaps the worst was over.

Let us make a quick analysis of what would happen in the months to come. We established that the current crisis started as a result of the failure of the consumer credit mechanism. As a result, bridging of the economic system gap began to fail. In fact, the crisis is continuing as of this day of writing because of the same reason.

Will the government decision to absorb bad debt of financial institutions help to revive the consumer credit mechanism to its former level? The answer is No.

Before the crash, the economic system gap had been mainly bridged by consumer credit. Consumer credit came from two main sources. One source was the banking sector. The other was the nonbanking sector on Wall Street. This second source played a prominent role in the past before the crash.

Now, as a result of the stock market crash, the second source of consumer credit mechanism is virtually paralyzed. Let us assume that because of the government's recent decision, the stock market calmed down and stock prices kept increasing. However, increasing stock prices cannot revive the failed "nonbank-centered" consumer credit mechanism, because bidding for stocks and investing in investment banks to enable them to supply credit are two different things.

Since the investors have lost faith in Wall Street financial institutions, those institutions will not be able to raise capital for the delivery of credit. Therefore, this component of credit delivery system will not be revived at least for another 10 to 15 years. Hence, now there is a vacuum in the consumer credit mechanism.

So, if banks are not geared up to fill the vacuum, the failure of the bridging of the economic system gap should continue in the months to come. However, banks themselves that have been severely beaten up by the crisis will restrain consumer credit delivery as a result of income fears on the part of their consumer clients.

In addition, criminal investigation into the high-ranking executives in failed financial institutions has installed a general fear among executives of all lending institutions, and, as a result, they might observe voluntary restrictions when issuing credits especially to consumers.

Government hands are becoming too tight because of their recent commitments to the stimulus package and to absorb unprecedented amount of bad debt. As a result, the government also cannot heavily increase deficit spending that would really help to increase the consumer income by way of undertaking public projects.

Added to the injury is that the people begin to think that if they save money by reducing consumption they can be ready to face the consequences individually. Consumer savings will widen the gap, thereby making bridging the gap more difficult.

Because of all these reasons, the bridging mechanism will continue to fail in the months to come. That means the worst is yet to come unless the general cancellation of consumer debt is carefully planned and executed safely.

Why should we do this? It is only because it is the methodology to revive the consumer credit mechanism that will ensure the filling of the economic system gap so as to ensure that the producer entrepreneurs will get back what they expect from the consumers out of their expenditure.

If this is not done, the production will be drastically reduced by entrepreneurs expecting to find equilibrium at a lower production level. That is a downward spiral toward a greater recession. In the event, the now-calmed stock market (if it is calm) will see another body blow shortly. In fact, what is at risk is the physical well-being of the members of society.

In an effort to enlighten people on this issue, on March 11, 2008, I wrote to the Federal Reserve Board, "Dear Sirs/Madams, economic theory rather than data will give you a much better understanding about how you should approach this crisis."

The said theory is proved and explained in this book. I suggest that the reader should read the chapters as they are arranged for a better and clearer understanding.

September 27, 2008

PART 1
THE THEORITICAL SETTING

PART 1
INTRODUCTION

We have a very practical question that has never been raised in economic studies so far.

The economic system produces a certain amount of products for consumption and a certain amount of products for the use of production. In a given period, if the value of what is produced for consumption is "X," and if the money paid to consumers for the same period is "Y," then can the Y be equal or greater than X? In other words, can the aggregate consumer income be greater than the value of consumption?

If the aggregate consumer income is greater than the value of consumption, consumers collectively can have a net saving; if not, consumers have to borrow the balance money or to find some other way to do their consumption.

The renowned British economist John Maynard Keyes wrote "when our income increases our consumption increases also, but not by so much." The reason is, he explained, "as a rule to a greater proportion of income being saved as real income increases." (The General Theory of Employment, Interest, and Money). This is a psychological law according to his exposition.

Ever since I read Keynes, I have been speculating as to whether we can apply this simple concept to the macro (national) level as envisaged by Keynes in his major theoretical work.

It is found that the aggregate consumer income is always less than the aggregate consumption at the macro level. As a result, although a certain number of consumers can save as their income increases, at no point can consumers as a collective group of people have a net savings under normal economic circumstances. Here the normal circumstances mean the absence of any significant trade surplus in the country.

Economists who believe consumer income is greater than the consumption would promote consumer saving, while others who believe consumer income is less than the value of consumption will promote consumers to borrow the balance of the money or find some other way to consume.

So, it is clear that the above question is not purely an academic one; instead, it is a most important practical question on the policy approach.

The above question leads to establish "the theory of economic system gap and credit cycle," which, in turn, established that the amount of money paid to consumers for their consumption is always less than the value of consumption as long as capital has continued to accumulate. Therefore, this book is in relation to this theory and its practical application to the economic system to have a better and more efficient economy within nation states and globally.

Yet, how do consumers as a collective group of people spend a sum of money equal to the value of consumption while having an income less than the value of consumption? The short answer is consumer credit. This is true as long as capital has continued to expand irrespective of the political structure. This means no matter how advanced (or rich) the economy is, consumers have to be in debt as long as capital has continued to accumulate. The best illustration is the United States. It is the richest country on earth, but consumers incur the highest debt.

However, in reality, it is quite natural that consumers save some money, which, in turn, widens the gap. Therefore, if some of the consumers save part of their income, others need to borrow more than what is saved and spend on consumption in order to put the economic system into equilibrium. To meet this situation, capitalism has evolved a system called fractional reserve banking, which could create more credits based on relatively fewer savings. Thus, in the economic system, saving is only a tool to create more credits. The notion that somebody's saving is absorbed by another, which many economists believe, is simply not true.

Because of the importance of the fractional reserve banking system in the economy, chapter 1 is dedicated to explaining the concept of it.

Karl Marx said, "The wealth of those societies in which the capitalist mode of production prevails, presents itself as an immense accumulation of commodities, its unit being a single commodity."

It is conceivable that this is relevant to socialist societies too, even though the ownership of means of production could be different from that of a capitalist society. Societies, whether capitalist, socialist or any other, need to produce goods and services known as commodities, and an abundance of them is referred to as wealth.

Yet, how could the production be done efficiently? What is the theory in relation to efficient production of wealth? Is economic efficiency linked to any political structure such as capitalist, socialist, or any other?

It has been found that the money-based production system, especially in relation to commodity production, has to behave in a unique and specific manner. That behavior is that it should be capable of maintaining a healthy gap between the aforementioned aggregate consumer income and the value of consumption, and this gap, which is defined as an economic system gap, need necessarily be filled mainly by consumer credit to ensure that the economic system is in equilibrium to facilitate capital accumulation.

Therefore, the question to be asked when the society is opting for a political system or choosing a souring ruler (king or queen) is as follows: Which is the political structure that would nurture this particular behavior best?

However, so far, capitalists have been proven to be more innovative than socialists or souring rulers. Therefore, we have a comparatively successful capitalist system that integrates this particular behavior into economic management.

Capitalists, without knowing what they are doing, attribute this relative success to individual greediness, justify it as human nature, and further promote it.

The reason why I mentioned that capitalists do not know what they do is because, as we shall see later, the comparative success in capitalism is mostly attributed to the evolution (or invention) of the fractional reserve banking system or the credit mechanism of filling the said economic system gap. Capitalist economists so far have not theoretically explained why they need fractional reserve banking system, yet they practice it, but we explain the reason very theoretically in this book.

If anybody wishes to challenge this notion, he or she can practically do it by implementing 100 percent reserve banking, which is a system that does not allow banks to create more credit than incoming deposits, and that system is quite contrary to fractional reserve banking.

If you do so, with all goodies of private property ownership, private entrepreneurship, and individual greediness, in capitalism, the economy is sure to dwindle to an unimaginable extent. This means it is not the pure capitalist structure that contributes to relative success, but there is an underlying deep reason for it.

Developed capitalist countries have been capable of maintaining a good economic system gap and filling it by credit primarily generated through the fractional reserve banking system. This is the very reason (absence of such arrangement) that some countries cannot thrive even with having physical potential and a basic capitalist structure.

However good the fractional reserve banking is, it brings its own contradiction into the system. The current global financial crisis (2008) surfaced because of this contradiction. Unless we understand the fundamental theory, we cannot uncover the bad implications. This knowledge is the key to reshaping our economic system.

Societies will move on until they find the ultimate efficient system in economic management that harmonizes people's needs with the sustainable resource use globally. The theory explained here will be useful in this effort.

CHAPTER 1
FRACTIONAL RESERVE BANKING

"One of the most knowledgeable financial writers in the USA thinks that the Federal Reserve's staff now do not have a very clear understanding of what they are doing or even what they think they are doing. Ironically, it would seem that as the monetary authorities have striven, in recent times, to make the system more transparent and subject to formal values of operation, it has become less intelligible" (Mayer 2001, as quoted by Ingham, 2004). The Federal Reserve Bank is the U.S. version of the Central Bank.

As the above quote described, the monetary system is understandably complex. Since it is complex, it is up to the economic theorists and not up to the practitioners to simplify it, as scientists usually do in their fields of interest, to enable the public to understand difficult phenomena.

Without understanding the mechanics of the monetary system, in fact, it is difficult to understand how the current economic system works in detail. Furthermore, some knowledge about fractional reserve banking would enable the reader to understand the core theory explained in this book.

This is the main reason to start this book explaining the fractional reserve banking system that we practice today.

Under the system of fractional reserve banking, the commercial banks create more money than printed by the government. The money thus created by commercial banks is known as "credit–money." We will learn this process very clearly in this chapter.

However, if the Central Bank is requested to provide the details on the stock of money, you will find out immediately that the stock of government printed notes and minted coins is well outnumbered by the stock of credit–money solely created by commercial banks through the system of fractional reserve banking.

The easiest way to understand this concept is through the following historical story.

In the middle centuries, goldsmiths started this practice. People deposited part of their gold with goldsmiths for safe keeping. The goldsmith then issued a note to the depositor. The goldsmith returned a person's gold on return of his note. Sometimes, they charged a small fee for his service payable by gold or silver.

When people wanted to borrow, they came to goldsmiths. Goldsmiths have deposits of other's gold, and knowing that each and every body would not withdraw all the gold deposited at any one time, he could lend gold from the deposits in his custody. Accordingly, the maximum he could loan out was the deposit he had. However, he had to keep a fraction of the deposits as a precautionary measure to return to the customer whenever a customer came to withdraw his or her deposit.

Since the note issued on the deposit was honored by the goldsmith, sometimes people used the notes to settle their payments among themselves. Now, the goldsmiths understood people are not withdrawing their gold at any one time, and his notes were considered as money—the gold.

Given this understanding, subsequently he decided to issue a note when people came to borrow gold to pay their debt or make payment to another. Since the note was exchangeable to gold when it was presented to the goldsmith, people liked it. It was easy to carry and handle too.

Because of this practice of the people, the goldsmith got an opportunity to lend more money in the form of notes than the gold he actually had to back up. If he had to lend gold, then he could lend only what he had. A goldsmith note was just a piece of paper. He could create any amount of them. So, he could lend any amount to borrowers in the form of notes. However, there were certain limits.

Let us take an example. People deposited 100 gold coins. At the remotest possibility, sometimes they withdrew 25 percent of it, which meant 25 gold coins. At such an occasion, the goldsmith could have only 75 coins in his custody at any given time. Taking this into consideration, the goldsmith could safely lend only 75 gold coins at any given time. In this scenario, he is liable to return 100 gold coins on demand, and that is his total liability.

Out of the total liability, he had to have 25 percent as actual gold reserve, because, according to his past experience, he knew that only 25 percent of deposits would be withdrawn at the remotest possibility.

Now, he realized two things. People liked his notes and used them to settle payments among them. In addition, he now knew that if he maintained 25 percent of actual gold reserve out of his total liability, he could continue the lending business without any problem.

Then, he thought if he was to keep all 100 gold coins as the reserve, then he could lend more money in the form of notes.

So, he decided to keep all 100 gold coins as the reserve. According to his estimates, he had to maintain only 25 percent of actual gold reserve out of his total liability. He knew it by experience. Therefore, he could now calculate what should be his total liability if he was to keep 100 coins as the reserve.

Let us calculate it. It is interesting and easy. Now, 25 percent of the total liability should be equal to 100, the actual gold reserve. We can use a simple mathematical equation to calculate total liability. If the total liability is X, then X × 25% = 100. Therefore, X = 400. That means total liability should be 400.

So, he now knows his total liability should not exceed 400 if he wants to continue his lending business uninterrupted in the event he kept all 100 gold coins as reserve. Already he had 100 actual gold deposits as liability. If he issues notes to borrowers to the value of 300, then his total liability would be 400. So, he can safely continue the lending business if he issues notes only to the value of 300. So, he did it, and his profits increased exponentially.

Now, depositors of 100 coins have notes to the value of 100. Borrowers too have 300 notes. Altogether, there are 400 notes perhaps in circulation. At the remotest possibility, sometimes only 25 percent of note holders will come to withdraw gold. Twenty-five percent of 400 equals to 100. So, the goldsmith had these 100 gold coins in his reserve. Virtually, he faces no problem.

What he did was he lent money he did not actually have. The total system depended on the trust people kept on the goldsmith.

Now, assume the rate of interest he charges is 8 percent. In the first scenario, he lent 75 gold coins. So, he can earn 6 gold coins at the rate of 8 percent interest. In the second scenario, he lends 300. He earns 24 gold coins at the rate of 8 percent interest. His income has quadrupled.

The first type of banking can be defined as savings banking or 100 percent reserve banking. The rule is the bank cannot lend more than what they have as incoming deposits.

The second type of banking is called fractional reserve banking. The rule is the bank should only maintain a fraction of real cash reserve to the total liability.

In those days, the reserve requirement was decided by the goldsmith. Today, this reserve requirement is specified by Central Banks and in the United States by the Federal Reserve Bank. As of now, the mandatory reserve requirement in the United States is at 10 percent.

Now, assume that the goldsmith could operate at a 10 percent reserve requirement. Let us do the math again. He had 100 gold coins. His reserve requirement should be 10 percent, and 10 percent of the total liability should be equal to 100, because he intends to keep all 100 gold coins as reserve.

Assume X is the total liability. Therefore, $X \times 10\% = 100$. So $X = 1,000$. Thus, total liability must be 1,000. Out of this total liability, already 100 coins are in the reserve and is a liability so that he could create another 900 credit in the form of notes that would become his liability. By doing that, he operates within the liability limit.

In addition, we can now calculate his interest income. He charges as usual 8 percent of interest. So, interest revenue should be $900 \times 8\%$. It comes to 72.

You will see his interest income is increased exponentially. This is exactly how today's commercial banks operate. They really do not make money on your deposits. These deposits are with them safely. However, they need your deposit to create credit multiple times. That is how they create money that they lend.

The notes issued by a goldsmith to borrowers were indistinguishable from the notes he issued to depositors. Now, there are an additional 900 notes in the circulation, which means the money supply has increased. Those notes are money substitutes, and new money is credit–money.

This is exactly the process now in practice in our economy by commercial banks. To create new money, the person who accepts the deposit should be able to create a money substitute. Only commercial banks can do it today. Their checks and money accounts act as money substitutes. A savings bank cannot create new money even if they accept deposits and lend money, because they do not operate checking (current) accounts. So, they cannot create a money substitute.

This effect was summarized by Graham Towers, former governor of the Central Bank of Canada. He said, "Each and every time a bank makes a loan; new bank credit is created—new deposits—brand new money."

However, this banking system is inherently bankrupt. Therefore, it needs a backup system to stabilize it. This is one of the jobs of the Central Bank. It has to stabilize the financial system. Let us take the same example of a goldsmith to understand it.

The goldsmith issued notes to depositors and borrowers. He maintained only 10 percent of actual cash reserve. That means only 10 percent of notes are backed by cash. There are another 900 notes in circulation without real cash to back them up.

So, assume all of the note holders or a good part of them came to the goldsmith to change his notes into cash, but he does not have enough real cash to pay. He is bankrupt. He has to close down the business.

However, now assume he had a friend or two who could lend part of their cash reserves to meet the demand of cash for a week or so. Because the goldsmith knows even though a good part of the notes were converted into gold, that gold would be deposited with him rather quickly for safe keeping. Therefore, the goldsmith borrowed money for the short term to pay for the withdrawals. However, he had to pay higher interest for such short-term borrowing from his friends. So, it is a very delicate balancing act that the goldsmiths had to play every day.

This is exactly what commercial banks do every day. They do bank-to-bank borrowing/lending, and the rate charged is higher than the normal rate, which is called the overnight borrowing rate.

If the whole banking system is in a liquidity crisis, then they go to the Central Bank. If the Central Bank does not have real reserves, then they just can create money. That is why fractional reserve banking cannot be sustained without the support of the Central Bank. This was amply demonstrated in the financial crisis of 2008 in the United States.

Although we explain the concept of today's fractional reserve banking in simple terms, it is a much more complex system and a little bit (not completely) safer because of regulatory measures and the ability of the Central Bank to bail out the system when it faces a crisis.

(Please note this historical story brought up here is only to explain the concept behind the fractional reserve banking system, but, in fact, it might have or might not have any value as a historical account.)

However, the above discussion is not complete unless we study different views held by authoritative individuals.

Most mainstream economists, it seems, did not understand this concept of fractional reserve banking and how it really affects the money creation process.

In addition, if we do not look into others' attempts to explain this concept and analyze them critically, readers of this book perhaps might not be convinced of the above explanation, because it is too profitable for the banks to believe it. Hence, I wish to submit authoritative sources' views held differently and analyze them.

Geoffrey Ingham wrote and published a monologue about money in 2004 entitled *The Nature of Money* (Ingham 2004). He had been attached to Cambridge University for over four decades. Because of his long career at the prestigious Cambridge University, I think it would be better to look at his views about credit–money and fractional reserve banking. His perception on this particular subject is different from what we discussed above.

He wrote as follows.

> During 1920s, it was beginning to realize that the banking system's pyramid of debts was itself a mean of producing new money. Banks accept deposits on which they pay interest, and these debts (liabilities to their creditors) form the basis of lending. However, banks also extend loans unmatched by incoming deposits. These create deposits against which cheques may be drawn and are debts owed to the banks (assets). These debts become money and find their way into other banks in the system. Banking practice has developed through conventions and regulations to the point where only a small fraction of deposits (liabilities) from creditor customers are kept as a reserve out of which to pay these depositors, should they wish to withdraw their money. As reserves earn no interest, banks strive to

operate with the smallest fraction they can. Assuming that a bank operates with a 10 percent fractional reserve, for every £100 deposited (liabilities), it is able to advance loans (assets) of £90. As it is spent, this monetized debt appears in bank accounts elsewhere in the system. In turn, further deposits are created against which these other banks may extend loans—in the first instance, a loan of £81 (£90 minus £9 (10 percent fractional reserve) = £81). Eventually initial deposit of £100 could produce £900 of new money in the form of loans. (Ingham 2004, p. 151)

Let us investigate this notion of fractional reserve banking and credit–money creation. The author says, "However, banks also extend loans unmatched by incoming deposits." This statement is not quite clear. If the bank accepts a deposit of £100 and extends a loan to another for £90, then it qualifies the above statement. In addition, if a bank accepts a deposit and extends a loan to another for £120, then such a scenario also qualifies the above statement.

Therefore, to verify what the author meant by the above statement, we can look into the example given. Now, when we look at the example the author brought forward to clarify the issue, we can see that the author is referring to the first scenario. In the example, the first bank accepts a deposit of £100. Since the bank operates under a 10 percent reserve requirement, usually imposed by the Central Bank, it has to keep £10 as reserve. So, the bank extended a loan to another customer for £90.

The loan extended is unmatched by the incoming deposit, but it does not exceed the incoming deposit; therefore, this should be the scenario he explained by the above statement. This is the only legitimate conclusion any student of economics could arrive at.

This is not fractional reserve banking, and it is not the banking practice that commercial banks are practicing today. This is 100 percent reserve banking, and it has no power to create money in credit form or otherwise.

However, the author in our above passage claims that eventually an initial deposit of £100 could produce £900 of new money in the form of loans. Can we create new money by a banking system explained in the passage? Let us investigate further.

We have a deposit of £100. The fractional reserve requirement is 10 percent. So, the bank keeps £10 as a reserve, and the balance of £90 is loaned out to another. Now, the borrower has £90, and bank has £10. If the bank opens a checking account for the borrower, then the bank keeps all £100, and a check amounting to £90 may be drawn by the borrower. If he drawn a check for £90 to pay for another that amount is well backed by the dollars in the bank. Whatever the case, this money did not increase.

Now, the first borrower settled a payment to another. That person deposited the £90 into his account in another bank. At this moment, let us take a stock of the money. The first bank has £10, the first borrower has nothing, the third person who deposited the £90 has nothing in his vault, and the second bank just got £90 as a deposit; altogether, it comes to £100. However, in the process, a credit of £90 is created, but it is well backed by the dollars or pounds in the banks or the system. Money is virtually not created.

Therefore, it is clear in this system of banking, credit is created, but money in the form of credit–money is not created.

What is fractional reserve banking? Everybody agrees that it is a system that could extend loans unlatching to incoming deposits but essentially exceeding the value of deposits. It can be presumed the above author also had the same idea when he wrote what he did, though the example given was wrong.

To understand this, let us go back to our middle century goldsmith.

We assume that we deposited $100 with our goldsmith. He accepts it and gives us a note. That is a note the community accepts as money, because, on returning it to the goldsmith, this one or any other will get $100. He is required to operate with a 10 percent reserve requirement.

This means to him that the Central Bank wants him to keep cash reserve amounting to 10 percent of his total liability.

He has two options. The accepted deposit is liability, and that amounts to $100. So, the first option is to keep $10 and loan out the balance of $90, as exemplified in the above passage.

The second option is, since he is smart, he decided to keep all $100 as reserve. Therefore, he now has to calculate what his total liability should be. It is simple. Out of the total liability, 10 percent should be equal to $100, which is the reserve amount. If total liability is X, then $X \times 10\% = \$100$. Therefore, X is equal to $1,000.

However, already he has a deposit of $100, and it is a liability. So, he can take the liability to another $900; both equal $1,000. Therefore, now he decided to issue notes to his borrowers amounting to the value of $900. This note is a liability to the goldsmith, because he has to honor it and provide cash on return. However, the loan owed to him by the borrowers is an asset to the goldsmith. He is earning interest on it.

In this case, he has not violated the Central Bank's rule, because he is maintaining a 10 percent reserve of his total liability. In this case, he practically did not loan out any money out of the deposit he received; instead, he created new credit–money amounting to $900 in the form of his notes.

This is the concept of fractional reserve banking and credit–money. Therefore, Ingham's above clarification does not explain the real system.

Instead of goldsmith notes, today you replace it with bank endorsable checks. If the bank cannot issue checks or another money substitute, then fractional reserve banking is not possible. Instead of goldsmith's notes—a virtual money substitute—today, checks are in circulation.

However, it is easily misunderstood that each credit will become money. It is not. Each and every bank cannot do this type of money creation and participate in fractional reserve banking. The first condition is that they should be able to create a money substitute that is equivalent to goldsmith notes. Commercial banks can do it.

Savings banks accept deposits and create credit too. However, most of them are not eligible to maintain checking accounts, which are the primary prerequisite to produce a money substitute. They maintain their account with other commercial banks. When they issue a loan, the check they write is drawn from its commercial banker, since they are not able to produce a substitute of money that could be put into circulation. As such, the point of the creation of money is not the savings bank, though they issue loans; instead, it is the commercial bank that can create credit–money using savings banks' deposits, which are in their accounts.

Technically, the banks that can participate in the fractional reserve banking system are designated as commercial banks.

CHAPTER 2
THE THEORY OF ECONOMIC
SYSTEM GAP AND CREDIT CYCLE

No country in contemporary history has ever become rich, and it cannot do so without maintaining an economic system gap and without filling it predominantly by consumer credit knowingly or unknowingly. If consumer credit was not created within the country, then it has to be done in some other second country—usually in the importing country—in order to become a country rich.

This phenomenon is explained through the theory of economic system gap and credit cycle, and, hence, it has a direct practical value in reshaping world economies. Let us investigate this matter.

An entrepreneur sells his output to a consumer or to another entrepreneur or to both. Accordingly, the contemporary economic system produces a certain amount of goods and services for consumption and certain products for the use of production.

Let us consider the consumption part. The economic system produces a certain amount of goods and services to sell to consumers. In addition, the economic system must pay a certain amount of money as income in order for the consumers to do the consumption.

Now, the important question is as follows. Can the economic system pay consumers an income in excess or equal to the value of consumption? We found out this is not possible no matter how rich the country is. Therefore, consumers have to borrow in order to consume. As superficial empirical evidence, we cite the example of the United States; it is considered as the richest country on earth and also carries the highest debt on the part of consumers. However, as we continue this analysis, we will find the true reason.

If the income of consumers as a collective group is less than the value of their consumption, then they have to borrow or some other way has to be found to put the economic system into equilibrium. The economic system must always be in equilibrium, which means what is offered for consumption is consumed by the community. Or more correctly, what could be consumed would be offered by the system.

Therefore, the question that is going to be explored is not a purely academic one; rather, it is perhaps the most important practical question in economics.

This chapter will analyze this issue—the issue of whether the economic system can pay the consumers enough money to do their consumption. If the system does not pay enough to consumers, what are the implications?

Let us take an example. If $500 is the capital used in the production and the value of the commodity output is $590, then original capital has now grown from $500 to $590. This surplus $90 is the expanded capital.

To make it simple, let us assume an economic system where entrepreneurs produce and sell directly to the consumer and employ labor only. That means nothing such as raw materials and machinery is bought from another entrepreneur. This type of economic system is called a fully integrated economic system.

Since the revenue is realized only from consumers in a fully integrated economic system, the value of consumer sales is $590 in our above example. In the same period, $500 is the amount paid to labor, which means to consumers. This includes the entrepreneur's own consumption.

So, the system offered something for $590 to consumers. This is the value of consumption that the entrepreneurs expect to get back from consumers out of their expenditure. However, consumers were paid only $500. That means the system is not in equilibrium. There is a gap between what is available for consumption, which is higher, and the consumer income. That gap is $90. This gap arises due to the requirement to provide for capital expansion, as we noticed above.

However, if this gap is not filled or if the system is not in equilibrium, then capital expansion does not occur. Therefore, consumers must have $590 to do their consumption. How do they get it? They get it as consumer credit. (There are several other methods, but, as we shall see later, they are neither important nor efficient.)

What does this mean? This means consumers have to be in debt as long as capital continues to accumulate. It is this consumer credit mechanism that puts the economic system into equilibrium.

Here we assumed that consumers spent all their income without saving any money or some households' savings were absorbed by another household's for the use of consumption. However, we saw there is still a gap that needs to be filled. In fact, the need for consumer credit exceeding consumer income or exceeding consumer savings arises due to the gap between consumer income and consumption. It is a gap we need to create in the economic system for the capital accumulation process. Richness of the country at any level has nothing to do with it.

This gap is a system gap, and, hence, it is defined as the economic system gap. As we shall see below, this same thing happens in the contemporary economic system that we live in today.

This is a system gap common to any economic system whether it is capitalism, socialism, or any other if the system is money based.

Please note here, one might argue that if the expanded capital of $90 is invested in the current period and the produce is not available to be sold in the same period, then the system should be in equilibrium, as $90 should go to labor—the consumers.

In that case, we should account for the sales realized in the current period arising from the investments of the previous period too. Therefore, it is reasonable to ignore both, only to understand the issue. In fact, investment widens the gap in the future and does not play any role in filling the gap. Instead, filling the gap promotes the accumulation of capital for new investments in the future.

Let us investigate further. Consider the same example given above. In the real world, labor saves a little bit of money too. Let the savings made collectively be $100. As a result, the said gap (here the gap should be understood as the gap to be created between after saving income and the value of consumption) increases to $190 from $90. Unless this gap is filled, the production cannot continue smoothly, because the economic system is not in equilibrium.

However, because of savings, now the bankers have $100 as deposits. They make consumer loans. Since they have only $100 as deposits, the maximum sum they can loan out is $100 according to common sense. Still, $90 is short to put the economic system back into equilibrium.

If the bankers can loan out $190 based on the deposit that they have (they have only $100), we can put the economic system into equilibrium. That means bankers have to create more credits based on relatively less savings.

In fact, modern capitalism evolved such a banking system and is called fractional reserve banking, which was discussed chapter 1. As we now know, it is a system of banking that creates more credit based on a little amount of deposits. By doing that, the fractional reserve banking system puts the economic system into equilibrium.

In fact, capitalism's relative success should be attributed to this consumer credit mechanism. That mechanism filled the economic system gap, thereby allowing capital accumulation to process faster.

Economists believe somebody's savings are absorbed by another as credit in the capitalist system. That is the common belief of most contemporary economists. This idea was well articulated by Sydney Weintraub as follows.

> "The capitalist system generates its dynamism in borrowing and lending—despite the wisdom of Polonius. The mechanics and validity of capitalism

repose in the transfer of funds from those reluctant to employ their current surplus to those eager to exploit lucrative opportunities in entrepreneurial uses, and willing to pay an interest price." (Weintraub 1978, p. 243)

However, this is only a partial truth. In fact, we proved above that the economic system can only be put into equilibrium by creating and providing more credit based on a little savings allowing accumulating capital. Therefore, in fact, capitalism's dynamism should only be attributed to this special credit creation mechanism exceeding savings.

If what Sydney Weintraub said above was true, then 100 percent reserve banking where banks could not create more credit than what they have as deposits could be appropriate. In fact, even Milton Friedman, the founder of monetarist school of economics, advocated 100 percent reserve banking. Though he was considered as the Karl Marx of capitalism, the economic practitioners are not listening to him on this particular issue.

However, so far, economic practitioners have not justified why they need fractional reserve banking. Above we understood why we cannot do away with fractional reserve banking, though improvements are welcome and needed.

From the above discussion, we have established following.

(1) The economic system cannot pay enough income to consumers to do the consumption of what is produced for consumption by the system when the economic system continues to accumulate capital. This is the first principle of economics.

(2) It is (mainly) by consumer credit that the economic system is put into equilibrium (definitely not by investments).

(3) The gap between consumer income and the value of consumption, which is already created due to the requirement of capital expansion, will be increased by consumer savings. As a result, we require a banking system to create more credit based on a little savings primarily to put

the economic system into equilibrium. The fractional reserve banking system caters to this fundamental requirement.

(4) Advocating 100 percent reserve banking has no rational basis.

In the above, we considered a fully integrated economic system. It is a hypothetical system. The economic system in which we live today is not fully integrated. It is an unintegrated economic system.

However, there is only one big difference between both systems that we should be concerned about in this analysis. In an unintegrated system, an entrepreneur could sell his product to a consumer or other entrepreneur, whereas in a fully integrated system, the producer bought nothing from another and sold his produce directly to the consumer.

Therefore, total sales in an unintegrated system do not represent the value of consumption, but in a fully integrated system, it does represent the value of consumption. Therefore, determination of the value of consumption is difficult in unintegrated economic system.

However, we can overcome this difficulty in quantifying consumption in an unintegrated economic system by defining it in a particular way, as we shall see below.

However, our above conclusions are still applicable to that system, because the difference is not in principle but in calculation. Therefore, we shall continue this discussion later after explaining the proof of economic system gap in an unintegrated economic system, based on the above example only for a matter of simplification.

Economic System Gap in Unintegrated Economic System

In an unintegrated system, during any period of time, entrepreneurs will sell the finished output to consumers or to other entrepreneurs for a certain sum, which we will designate as A. Let us designate the amount sold to other entrepreneurs as A1.

Entrepreneurs will also have spent a certain sum, designated as A2, on purchasing output from other entrepreneurs. This includes all costs such as raw materials, utility, and cost of machinery incurred by producing A except labor employed by the entrepreneur.

In addition, entrepreneurs spend a certain sum employing labor to produce A. Let us designate the cost of labor as L, which includes cost of labor of all kinds, including any remuneration paid to the entrepreneur for his consumption.

Now, we can calculate the capital used on producing the output A. Capital used up is equal to A2 + L.

Let us now define the consumption. Expenditure on consumption during any period must mean the value of goods sold to consumers during that period. In other words, it is the value of goods purchased by consumer purchasers excluding purchases made by investor purchasers.

It is conceivable that it is not an easy task to differentiate consumer purchaser and investor purchaser.

"But this difficulty can be overcome when the consumption is defined as Σ (A − A1) where ΣA is the total sales and ΣA1 is total sales made by one entrepreneur to another. When we omit Σ we can write consumption as (A − A1)" (Keynes 1964, p. 62).

Anyway, this is just common sense. An entrepreneur sells his product either to consumers or to other entrepreneurs. Then, if we deduct from total sales the amount sold to other entrepreneurs, we will get what is sold to consumers. That is exactly what Keynes did above in defining consumption.

So, after defining the above two quantities, we can begin our analysis.

Since the entrepreneur wishes to receive a higher income than the capital used up, we can write:

A > (A2 + L)

where A is the total proceeds or income from the standpoint of entrepreneurs. (A2 + L) is the total capital used up in a given period.

Then, (A – A2) > L
(A – A2) – L > 0   (1)

Both A and A1 are two unambiguous book keeping quantities. Consumer sales are not in books. That is why we define consumption through two calculable quantities. That is the logic behind the above definition of consumption. We need to define consumption and consumer income in calculable form in order to compare them.

In addition, in calculating the capital used up, we need to know what is bought from another entrepreneur. We defined that quantity as A2, and it is also an unambiguous book keeping quantity.

In fact, when we take one entrepreneur, both A1 and A2 are in his books, but, when summed up separately at the macro level, both are equal. Because A1 of entrepreneur X is posted in the books of buyer entrepreneur Y as A2. Similarly, A2 of entrepreneur X is posted in the books of Y or any other as A1. Therefore, $\Sigma A1 = \Sigma A2$. When we omit Σ, we have A1 = A2.

From the above inequality equation (1), we know (A – A2) – L > 0. Since A1 = A2, we can write (A – A1) – L > 0   (2)

We know from above, (A – A1) is the value of consumption and L is consumption money made available by all entrepreneurial activity or consumer income. Therefore, inequality equation (2) tells us that the value of what is available for consumption is greater than the money paid for consumers by all enterprises. There is a gap between consumer income and the value of consumption.

Please note that this is the same gap we identified in the fully integrated economic system earlier.

Economic System Gap

The said gap should exist in any economic system if the economic system is money based. Therefore, I define this gap as the economic system gap. The gap arises from the need to expand capital immaterial of ownership of it or the entrepreneurs' requirement to receive a higher income than the capital invested. $(A - A1) - L$ is the economic system gap, and it is always greater than zero.

However, if the consumers did not purchase what is produced for consumption, then the production cannot continue, as the economic system is not in equilibrium. Therefore, the consumer liquidity must be equal to the value of consumption.

As we know, in the real world, some people save part of their income. As a result, the economic system gap increases. At the same time, some people take credit for consumption.

However, in order for the economic system to be in equilibrium, consumption must be equal to consumer liquidity or the amount they spent; as such, we can write:

$(A - A1) = L - s + cr.$
where s = consumer savings and cr = consumer credit.
Then, $(A - A1) - L = cr. + s$ (3)

Above, we saw that $(A - A1) - L$ is greater than zero (inequality equation 2). Therefore, the left-hand side of the above inequality equation (3) must be greater than zero. Therefore, the right-hand side of the above inequity must be greater than zero too.

Then, we have $cr. + s > 0$
$cr. > s.$

This simple inequity equation tells us that consumer credit must be greater than consumer or household savings in order to put the economic system into equilibrium. In other words, in order to facilitate the capital formation, the economic system has to create more consumer credit than savings. How do we do it? We do it through the fractional reserve banking system. Will the 100 percent reserve banking do this task? The answer is never. (Here we disregard the traditional definition of "national/domestic savings," since that term is deceptive. Savings on corporate balance sheets are not consumer savings, and they are not available for consumers as they want it).

Accordingly, we now see that the economic system gap exists in unintegrated economic system, and the fractional reserve banking system is required to fill the gap. As such, all conclusions made regarding the fully integrated economic system also are still applicable in terms of the not fully integrated system, although calculations differ.

Therefore, we shall now continue our investigation further with the original example that we considered at the beginning of this discussion. If $500 is the capital used in the production and the value of the commodity output is $590, then the original capital has now grown from $500 to $590. This surplus $90 is the expanded capital.

Now, the entrepreneur has expanded his capital by $90. He invests that in the next production cycle. He expects to receive higher revenue than what is invested. He realizes his revenue at the point of sale to the consumer, nowhere else.

So, the total capital he invested in the second period is $590, and, he realized, we shall assume, $696. (Here, we assumed he expected to have a same rate of return for his capital as in the previous production cycle.)

Now, the consumption amounts to $696, and money paid to do the consumption is $590. The gap is $106. What happened? The gap between consumer income and the value of consumption increased from $90 in the first period to $106 in the second period. That means even though consumer income increased due to increased economic growth, the gap widened.

However, it is not a problem; we have the fractional reserve banking system to provide consumer credit literarily for any amount, so the system continues, and we create more products and jobs. Community's income would grow, more borrowing would become possible, and it would create more capital.

However, the process comes to a breaking point if the consumers did not borrow to consume. Therefore, we are forced to consume, thereby exceeding our means to keep the system going.

That means the money-based economic system has put us (people) into a very unique behavior, where we have to borrow to consume to hold on to our jobs and create new ones for our children. If consumers do not borrow, then the economic system gap will not be filled, and, as a result, production would be discouraged and the economy would go into a recession or even into a depression.

This unique behavior is created from the system gap—the gap between consumer income and the value of consumption. (This is the true economic reason behind extreme consumerism which cannot be stopped by promoting individual savings. If the society can satisfy at lower production level then it can be achieved only through monetary and fiscal policy adjustments, not by promoting people to live within their means).

Credit can fill the gap between consumer income and the value of consumption, but it is temporary, and the contradiction in the economic system is far from over.

It brings much more contradictions, which need to be resolved, as it continues. Let us investigate further.

(Macro) Credit Cycle

Once again, let us take the same example. The entrepreneur invested $500 and expanded his capital to $590. Now, the entrepreneur has expanded his capital by $90. He invests that in the next production cycle. He expects to receive higher revenue than what is invested. He realizes his revenue at the point of sale to the consumer, nowhere else.

So, the total capital he invested in the second period is $590, and, he realized, we shall assume, $696. (Here we assumed he expected to have a same rate of return for his capital.) Now, the consumption amounts to $696, and money paid to do the consumption is $590. The gap is $106. The gap between consumer income and the value of consumption increased from $90 in the first period to $106 in the second period.

Therefore, it is clear as capital accumulation continues, then the gap between consumer income and consumption increases requiring consumers to borrow more collectively. However, this cannot continue forever. Because consumer debt can never be paid as a cumulative sum, it continues to accumulate instead. Therefore, the ratio of cumulative consumer debt to income increases. As a result, there should come a point where consumers cannot borrow any more money without defaulting on loans.

Let us consider the same example above to understand this process. Our entrepreneur invested $500, produced a product whose value is $590, and sold it to consumers. So, he paid only $500 to labor, that means to consumers requiring consumers to borrow $90 in order to purchase the product whose value is $590. In this case, the debt-to-income ratio is 90/500 × 100, and it comes to 18 percent. In the second cycle, he invested $590 and produces a product whose value is $696. In this case, he paid $590 to consumers. Out of this income, consumers have to pay the previous debt of $90 (forget about the interest). So, now they have only $500 to purchase a product whose value is $696. So, consumers need to borrow $196 in this case. Therefore, now the debt-to-income ratio is 196/590 × 100, and it comes to 33.22%.

Accordingly, we can see that ratio of cumulative debt to income increases even though consumer credit fills the gap. As a result, as this process continues, there comes a point where consumers cannot borrow any more money without defaulting on their loans, because their income is not sufficient to pay the previous loans.

Perhaps, one might ask, why did we not consider the ratio of cumulative debt to cumulative income? The consumer income spent on consumption is not cumulative. Once the consumption is done, then the consumer income is evaporated or has gone into some other's hand, namely entrepreneurs. Therefore, consumer income is not cumulative, but consumer debt is cumulative. That is why we should ignore cumulative income in our calculation.

As a result, after a period of growth, consumers are compelled to live within their means because of their shear inability to borrow and because of the lenders unwillingness to lend. However, we saw above, when consumers try to live within their means, then the economic system gap is not filled, and a recession should commence.

Beyond this point, until consumers' borrowing power is revived, the economy cannot expand; it cannot even stay stagnant, though physical productive power exists. The only option to prevent a recession and expand the economy beyond this point is to cancel part of the consumer debt. That means we have to abandon the old credit cycle when its historic duty is over and start a new one.

If we do not do it proactively, still we have to do it after a major destruction of physical productive power through a recession or a depression. Even going through a recession or depression, it has no ability to correct itself, as some economists prefer to think, including former U.S. Federal Reserve Chairman Alan Greenspan. In regard to the current (2008) economic recession, he suggested the government should not intervene by saying, "It will prolong agony," believing that it would correct itself.

Those who believe the economy can correct itself now must answer how the economy can adjust by itself to fill the economic system gap when the consumers cannot borrow any more as a result of the accumulated debt as they did before.

Accordingly, we now understand that the credit cycle has a lifespan. Lifespan of a credit cycle perhaps can be extending from a quarter to a half century. This explains the theory of the credit cycle.

Though most economists believe that the current (2008) world economic crisis originated from a housing mortgage meltdown in the

United States, truly, the present crisis marks the end of a macro credit cycle that started in late 1970s, and the mortgage crisis was only the immediate cause. The salient feature should be that the cumulative consumer debt-to-income ratio is so high that it prevents consumer borrowing. However, official economists still do not work on this important ratio.

Therefore, this crisis cannot end until the borrowing power of consumers is revived. This cannot be done at the current price and wage levels. To revive the consumer borrowing power in general, we need to allow for moderate inflation to set in and to make corresponding wage adjustments. What does this mean? This is the process of partial cancellation of debt in general in order to revive the consumer borrowing power again to go for another credit cycle.

However, there are at least two reasons to shorten the lifespan of a credit cycle. One is over accumulation of excess liquidity, and the second is the trade deficit, which we will discuss now.

Excess Liquidity

Let us take the same above example. An entrepreneur invests $500. He now understands that consumers are going to get credit. So, he arranges credit to buy the produce. As such, now instead of selling his produce at $590, he will be able to sell the produce at $610. However, actually, he needs only $90 as expanded capital. Now, he has extra $20. Let us call this extra money as "excess liquidity," and it owns to entrepreneur. Anybody who has bought a plot of land to build a house on financing understands this process.

When the entrepreneur sells his product at $590, only to have expanded productive capital of $90, then the economic system does not create any excess liquidity. When he sells the produce at $610, then it creates excess liquidity, and, as a result, the consumers' need for credit to fill the economic system gap increases.

Therefore, we can safely define "excess liquidity" as the money that is not required for consumption or capital as at a current price level. The term capital needs a small clarification. Money is not capital. Money has at least two useful interchanging forms. One is consumption mode, when consumers make purchases. The other form is money capital, where money becomes capital at the point of purchasing factors of production.

Over accumulation of excess liquidity is a byproduct that originated as a result of filling the economic system gap by credit. However, if we can remove the excess liquidity on a continuous basis, then there cannot be over accumulation of it, and production should continue, subject to the limit of physical capacity.

As a result of generating excess liquidity, as we saw above, the amount of credit needed to fill the economic system gap increases. As a result, that will increase the cumulative debt-to-consumer-income ratio. It is conceivable that a higher cumulative debt-to-income ratio can quicken the collapse of a credit cycle earlier.

Trade Deficit

Again, let us take our earlier example. An entrepreneur sells his products valued at $610. Earlier, he paid $500 to labor (i.e., consumers). Now, he decides to produce half of the production with $250 and to import the other half. So, he pays $250 to domestic labor, and he values the produce at $305 to have the same rate of return. Balance of goods is imported at a reduced price, for example $150, and he sells it at $205 again to have the same rate of profit.

Now, the total value of consumption is reduced from $610 to $510 (305 + 205). At the same time, the amount paid to domestic labor for consumption is reduced from $500 to $250. The economic system gap in the previous occasion was $110 (610 – 500), and now it is $260 (510 – 250) even though the value of consumption became cheap. Now, in this case of importing scenario, consumers in the United States need more credit than before.

Although in the above example we assume zero exports, this is exactly what happens with a huge trade deficit. With a huge trade deficit, the gap between consumer income and the value of consumption should increase, needing higher credit.

In such a situation, the credit cycle cannot sustain for a long time, because, again, the cumulative consumer-debt-to-income ratio is higher at a huge trade deficit. That means, with other factors in the economic system, a huge trade deficit recorded in the United States in past decades quickens the end of the credit cycle, which resulted in the current (2008) crisis. Accordingly, we can conclude that free international trade or fair trade is all meaningless rhetoric. Only balanced trade can be sustained.

So, we noticed above, excess liquidity and trade deficit quicken the crash of the credit cycle.

Bridging the Economic System Gap

Although, so far, we consider only consumer credit as a tool to fill the economic system gap, there are other tools that have been used in particular times of economic history or are being used presently. Let us now try to understand what those tools are.

Here we are intended to discuss the all-available tools to bridge the gap in brief.

Provision of Free Money to Consumers

In 1972, the U.S. government sent a check to almost every household in the United States and declared it as a tax rebate. In fact, in that year, the U.S. government did not balance the budget in order to provide a tax rebate. However, consumers got extra money at no cost. That money came outside the production process. The point here is that it helped to bridge the gap to a certain extent.

So, one way of bridging the gap is to provide free money by the institution that holds the monopoly to create money. In fact, what is necessary to bridge the gap is extra money not credit. Provision of free money could be one of them.

The same tax rebate mechanism was used once again to prevent a recession, which happened while writing this book in 2008. However, as we saw from our above analysis, a tax rebate is only a patch work. It could work if the consumers are facing a small credit crunch. Such a rebate would not work beyond a point if consumers are overburdened by debt.

When the tax rebate was extended, the government declared that the stimulus package would boost the consumption and expand the economy, thereby resulting in greater tax revenue in the future so that what is borrowed now could be paid by that time. This is a total fallacy.

Tax is consumption money allocated to the government originating from entrepreneurial activity. (We shall see this argument in detail in part 2 of this book). We saw above how despite how much the revenue is increased, the economic system cannot allocate enough consumption money to do the consumption. Tax is only a tool to distribute what is allocated for consumption by the system. Therefore, the rationale behind a tax rebate is meaningless, though the tax rebate helps to bridge the economic system gap marginally. In fact, a tax rebate is a kind of deficit spending, which we will discuss below.

Provision of Consumer Credit

In theory, what consumers need is extra money, because, as we saw above, the gap is a creation of the economic system and is no fault of the consumers. However, the society requires responsible consumption by its members. Free extra money does not create that sense of responsibility, but credit does.

Credit gives a sense of responsibility to consumers to choose his or her consumption priorities, because products are limited and made with limited resources. Now, the consumers know their liquidity is limited and would have to pay back whatever credit they take in the future.

However, if this is felt as a burden, then consumers would abstain from taking credit. If that happened, economic activity would be contracted. Therefore, this sense of responsibility is required only to the extent that it would ensure that the social produce would be consumed fully without chaos.

Now, remove the credit from the equation. Could any country utilize its physical productive power? Never!

Therefore, consumer credit is a good way of bridging the gap rather than providing free money from time to time.

Deficit Spending

Deficit spending is defined as the money expended by government to bridge its budget deficit.

As we shall see in part 2 of this book, the government draws its income from total consumption money allocated by enterprises by way of taxes. It is not important whether these taxes are deducted directly from enterprises or partly from enterprises and partly from employees.

Enterprises can pay it directly to the government or enterprises can pay that amount to employees and can let the employees pay it to the government. Usually, as in today's practice, both happen. However, this money is consumption money and should be paid to the government, and the government, in turn, should pay its employees to do their consumption.

Now, assume the government decided to undertake another project that required extra money outside its income. So now, there is a deficit in the budget, and extra money expended falls into the category of deficit spending. It can be a construction of a university or any other matter. However, the government has no money to do it. The government undertakes this project and would pay a new set of employees during the construction process. To do that, the government needs to bring extra money and, with that money, it needs to produce a new category of consumers. This will contributes to bridging the gap.

So, deficit spending is one way of bridging the economic system gap.

Investment of Self-Expanded Capital and Producer Credit

In the recovery of capital from total proceeds, we noticed above that part is allocated for expansion. When this is invested, a new group (new employees and their dependents) would become consumers. That contributes to bridge the gap in the period that is being invested.

In addition, credit is issued to new producers of both kinds, namely consumer goods producers and higher-order goods producers. Higher-order goods producers produce goods to be utilized by consumer goods producers. Before commission of their sellable production, they convert part of the capital advanced into consumption money. It creates a new group of active consumers, and their income, including possible credit, could contribute to bridging the gap.

This action is very similar to the government's deficit spending. However, in this case, when production of new enterprises comes in the future, that would widen the gap. However, this process should continue until the work force is fully employed.

So, investment is another way of bridging the gap today, but it creates a greater gap tomorrow, since all investments are to be recovered, in the final analysis, through consumer sales. Therefore, investment of self-expanded capital and investments made with producer credit could not strictly be regarded as a tool to bridge the economic system gap under normal circumstances.

Making Money from Money for Consumption (Stock Market)

Mr. Allen Greenspan, the ex U.S. Federal Reserve chairman, once said that out of each $4 invested in the stock market, $1 goes into consumption. When the prices of stocks increase, investors sell their stocks. In the process, they make some gains and part of it is utilized for the consumption. Let us assume we buy a car for personal use. However, it is not certain whether Greenspan meant this type of consumption or consumptions made through credit instruments in the capital market or both.

If he meant consumptions made through credit instruments extended by financial markets in the above statement, then we can disregard it here, because we already discussed it under the category of consumer credit. However, if consumption is made through the so-called capital gain by buying and selling of stocks, that is what we consider here.

In the stock market, you make money out of money through a bidding process but do not produce any service or product to satisfy any human need.

Yet, the stock market is a mechanism to provide money for consumption to bridge the gap. However, as we shall see later, this is a game that could be played by excess liquidity owners and not available for the majority of the consuming community and, hence, not considered as an efficient and effective tool.

Credit Card

In developed countries, one of the important consumer credit tools is a credit card. This is not a new tool, but it falls into the category of consumer credit.

Other Tools

Perhaps, readers might find novel tools of bridging the gap. It might be curious to investigate them. Interest income could be one of them, but those interests finally add up to the cost of goods, making no real impact in bridging the gap.

Conclusion

In view of what was discussed above, we have now established that no country in contemporary history could ever became rich, and it will never become rich without maintaining an economic system gap and without filling it predominantly with consumer credit, knowingly or unknowingly. So far, the history of the economy is that this gap is maintained and bridged unknowingly or by a trial-and-error methodology.

The Wright brothers produced the first airplane by the trial-and-error methodology, and they flew in the sky. However, today, we use the principles of aerodynamics in airplane design, and the vast progress achieved is attributed to that scientific methodology.

Similarly, understanding the theory of the economic system gap and credit cycle is the first step to restructure the economies of developing countries and the global economy as a whole on a sustainable path.

CHAPTER 3
CRITIQUE OF KEYNESIANISM

John Maynard Keynes, a renowned British economist, came close to identifying the gap we discussed in the previous chapter. However, because of a great irrational assumption, he missed the target, and that led him to a very wrong analysis.

We established two things in the theory of the economic system gap:

(1) The gap is defined as a gap between consumption and the money made available for consumption by all entrepreneurial activity.

(2) The said gap originates as a result of the legitimate requirement of the entrepreneur or the society to ensure an excess income over the capital invested.

On the contrary, Keynes defined a gap as the gap between aggregate supply price and consumer spending. He also attributed its origin to the psychological characteristics of consumers and, hence, could not define or explain one of the most important phenomena in the money-based economic system.

Keynes said, "When our income increases our consumption increases also, but not by so much. The key to our practical problem is to be found in this psychological law. For it follows from this that the greater the volume of employment the greater will be the gap between supply price (Z) of the corresponding output and the sum (D1) which the entrepreneurs can expect to get back out of the expenditure of consumers. Hence, if there is no change in the propensity to consume, employment cannot increase, unless at the same time D2 is increasing so as to fill the increasing gap between Z and D1." (Here D2 is defined as the investment. Please refer to pages 29 and 30 of *The General Theory of Employment, Interest and Money* by John Maynard Keynes (Keynes 1964).

The above statement, which many economists take for granted, merits thorough investigation as it is relevant to our main topic, the theory of economic system gap.

Keynes talks about a gap between aggregate supply price and the sum that the entrepreneurs expect to get back out of the expenditure of consumers and the need to fill this gap. Primarily, this is a gap that the economic system does not require to fill, and, secondly, this gap can never be filled by increased investment (D2) or by any other means.

To understand these points clearly, we must know the definitions of both parameters precisely.

One parameter is the sum (D1) that the entrepreneurs can expect to get back out of the expenditure of consumers. According to Keynes' definition, D1 is not the aggregate demand that consists of both consumer and investor purchases; rather, it is the aggregate or total consumer spending in a given period, which is money spent on consumption only. Entrepreneurs expect consumers to spend a maximum sum equivalent to the value of consumption offered. Therefore, the maximum value we can assign to D1 must be equal to the value of consumption offered by entrepreneurs.

Now, in macroeconomics, we know how to calculate consumption. Keynes explained it this way, "Expenditure on consumption can be unambiguously defined as $\Sigma (A - A1)$ where ΣA is the total sales made during the period and $\Sigma A1$ is the total sales made by one entrepreneur to another" (Keynes 1964, p. 62). This is a fair definition on which most economists agree. We can omit Σ for convenience. Then, $(A - A1)$ is the consumption.

Anyway, this is common sense. An entrepreneur sells his output either to a consumer or to another entrepreneur. Then, out of the total sales, what is not sold to another entrepreneur is what is sold to the consumer, and it is the value of consumption. We get it by deducting A1 from A.

So, the value of consumption is (A – A1), and this is the value Keynes defined above.

Therefore, the value of consumption that is (A – A1) must be equal to the maximum value of D1, because entrepreneurs expect consumers to spend what they have offered for consumption.

Now, let us define the other parameter, namely aggregate supply price (Z). "In simple terms aggregate supply price (Z) is the total proceeds (income) from the entrepreneurs' standpoint" (Keynes 1964, p. 24). In other words, it is the total sales made during the period; therefore, it is the same quantity defined as "A" above.

Therefore, we have now defined both parameters in comparable mode. Supply price is Z and is equal to A. The entrepreneurs expect to get back a maximum sum from consumers equal to consumption that is at its highest value D1 = (A – A1).

It is simple mathematics that A > (A – A1). Then, Z > D1.
So, there is a gap between A and (A – A1) and between Z and D1.

Since A is greater than (A – A1), there is an obvious gap, because consumption is only a part of total sales or the aggregate supply price. Similarly, at the highest value of D1, still D1 must constitute a part of Z. Then, you cannot ever fill this gap between A and (A – A1) or between Z and D1.

Can you imagine a situation where you would want to increase the consumption to total sales or bring down total sales to the level of consumption in order to fill the gap between two parameters? Never! The economic system does not want to fill this gap.

In addition, we cannot fill this gap by increasing investment. If anyone thinks of filling this gap, the only way to do it is by bringing the A1 equal to zero, which means the investor purchases should be zero. Then, it is a completely integrated economic system in which no entrepreneur purchases from another entrepreneur. Each entrepreneur produces and sells directly to the consumer. Keynes never wanted or suggested such a thing.

Then, what could have been the actual gap with practical importance that he was talking about? There are several clues. First, it is a gap that needs to be filled. Second, it originates because there is no spending of part of the income by consumers. Third, this gap can be filled by increased investments. Let us investigate these clues.

The economic system produces a certain amount of commodities for consumption. As we noticed above, consumption is defined as (A − A1). If consumers do not spend money on consumption, then the system cannot keep on producing, and, as a result, employment cannot increase too. That means consumers have to spend an amount equivalent to (A − A1) (i.e., the value of produce available for consumption). Then, this is the amount that entrepreneurs expect to get back out of the expenditure of consumers, which Keynes defined as D1.

Now, let us assume because of whatever reason consumers want to spend a smaller amount than what is available for consumption. If that happens, then it creates a gap between consumption and D1, which is essential to be filled in order to put the economic system into equilibrium. Obviously, investment is one way to fill it temporarily if the new investment is not going to be recovered through consumer sales in the current period. Is this the gap Keynes was talking about?

Let us examine further. He says as income grows, the community saves a little bit more and, as a result, now spends relatively less money on consumption. In other words, he says as income grows, it creates a gap between consumption (in fact, what is available for consumption) and what consumers are willing to spend on consumption. Now, the value of D1 is less than (A − A1). Then, it is clear this is a gap that must be filled in order to put the economic system into equilibrium.

Therefore, it is clear, in fact, that he was talking about a gap between consumption and the money consumers spend on consumption. It fits his entire criterion; this gap needs to be filled, this gap could also be increased by consumer savings, and this gap can be filled by increased investments temporarily. If so, this is the gap we defined as an economic system gap.

Definitely, it cannot be the consumer spending and supply price.

From all these arguments, we can safely conclude that the only gap Keynes was talking about as practically important is a gap between D1 and some other quantity. That other quantity is the value of consumption (i.e., (A – A1)). Then, this is the gap we defined as an economic system gap. Presenting it as a gap between D1 and Z is very wrong and has no practical value.

How does this gap arise? In short, the gap could occur because of two reasons. First, as Keynes assumed, it could take place by increased savings as income grows. Second, it could occur by not providing consumers enough money for consumption by all entrepreneurial activity.

Take the first case. In order for this case to be true, we must assume that consumers get an income equal or in excess of the value of consumption. When consumers save, leaving them to spend D1 less than (A – A1), the gap is created. Since consumers are paid by enterprises, Keynes might have assumed that the economic system is capable of paying to consumers a sum above or equal to (A – A1). That is exactly what he did. Look at the way he justified this assumption. He says that people increase consumption as income grows but not by so much. Based on this simple observation, he generalizes this situation to a macro level.

One might argue that there are people who increase their consumption more than income as their income grows, because they can borrow more as their income grows. This argument also could generalize to the macro level.

The second methodology above is wrong and so is Keynes's methodology. In addition, if Keynesian economists think he is right, then they also have to prove that the community receives an income equal to or higher than the value of consumption in order to create the gap by increased savings.

On the contrary, in this book, it is proved that the economic system is not capable of paying consumers enough money for consumption by all entrepreneurial activity; hence, create a gap between consumer income and the value of consumption offered.

Even if consumers spend all their income to consume, entrepreneurs do not get what they expect to receive from consumers—that value being $(A - A1)$. That is where consumer credit plays the role in bridging the gap and putting the economic system into equilibrium.

I proved this gap arises not due to any savings but due to the societal requirement to expand capital. Hence, it cannot be attributed to any psychological characteristic of consumers as Keynes did. It is a system gap.

Economists who criticize Keynes or disagree with him just overlooked this great error.

In addition, most politicians and economists believe Keynesian economics suggest government intervention to boost the economy during difficult times. This is only a sundry observation of Keynes. However, we theoretically explained in the previous chapter that the government's deficit financing would help to bridge the economic system gap. When the other bridging mechanisms are not effective, the government can intervene by deficit financing, spending money on public projects, or providing a "fake" tax rebate directly to consumers, as was done in the United States in 2008. In both cases, it contributes to bridging the gap. That is how we should look into the government's deficit financing.

However, primarily difficult times are the times when the bridging mechanisms of the economic system gaps have failed. This is when corrective measures are needed. Deficit financing is only one tool. All available tools were discussed in chapter 2.

The analytical economics of Keynesian theory is wholly based on the said erroneous presumption, and an approach based on that presumption. When those are disproved, there is no basis for Keynesian theory to stand on.

CHAPTER 4
TERMINAL RECESSION OF 2008

In this chapter, we explain the reasons for economic recession and the financial crisis of 2008 through the theory of economic system gap.

The crisis triggered in the latter part of 2007 in the United States. Many economists wrongly believed that the crisis resulted from the problems of the subprime housing market in the United States. Essentially, this is what was said by Ben S. Bernanke, the chairman of Federal Reserve Board, before the congressional budget committee on January 17, 2008. He said, "Heightened investor concerns about the credit quality of mortgages, especially sub-prime mortgages with adjustable interest rates, triggered the financial turmoil." (Bernanke's full testimony can be found in Annexure 1.)

On the contrary, I pointed out that this was a different kind of crisis and invented the term "terminal recession" to define it. I used the term "terminal recession" to define that beyond a certain point of economic growth, the economy cannot remain as it is or grow any further without canceling a good part of the consumer debt. On January 22, 2008, I wrote to Federal Reserve Board, and said, "We have come to that point." (I did not use the term "terminal recession" in that letter.)

From the theory of economic system gap, we now know that during periods of economic growth, the economic system gap has been bridged, while during major recessions, the bridging mechanism has failed.

Knowingly or unknowingly, the economic system gap is primarily set to be bridged by consumer credit. Therefore, any failure of the consumer credit mechanism should trigger a major recession. That is what began to happen in late 2007 in the United States. All other economic ills are just ramifications, not the cause. My repeated efforts to enlighten the Federal Reserve Board to this reality went unheeded.

Had the government and Federal Reserve Board realized that the recession stemmed from the failure of bridging the economic system gap, they could have invented better monetary and fiscal policies to revive the bridging mechanism to stop the whole crisis.

Though I did not have any concrete data by mid-2007, I realized that the consumer credit mechanism, which is now mostly "nonbank centered," was about to fail. By 2007, home foreclosures had been increasing, and some reports suggested home foreclosures could surpass two million at the end of 2007. Another analysis pointed out that over 50 percent of credit card holders in the United States had delayed payments. On the operational level, those were clear signals for over indebtedness of private consumers.

The government, the largest institutional consumer, also was really over indebted.

Those were clear indicators that private consumer borrowing and deficit financing would be drastically reduced. Through the theory of economic system gap and credit cycle, we clearly established that the most important tools to bridge the gap between consumer income and the value of the consumption are consumer credit and deficit financing.

By the end of 2007, both mechanisms to bridge the system gap were badly constrained. For this simple reason, in my above letter, I wrote to the Federal Reserve Board, "Both people and government cannot borrow as has been done before. When consumers do not borrow or the lenders cannot supply consumer credit, capital expansion does not occur resulting first stagnation and then recession."

Therefore, by the end of 2007, I, equipped with good theory, clearly realized the looming crisis should be a terminal recession. That means without cancellation of a good part of the consumer debt, it would not be possible to revive the consumers' ability to borrow, which is indispensable in bridging the economic system gap.

I made my perception known to the Federal Reserve Board, which communication they acknowledged.

On January 21, 2008, I wrote the following to the Federal Reserve Board. "Therefore the only solution is that we have to revive the borrowing power of consumer. To do that, we need to wipe off part of current overburden consumer debt. As at now only way to do it is to let the moderate inflation set in and at the same time make an adjustment to wage structure. We hate inflation but amazingly this is a situation where moderate inflation can save us. Accordingly even though U.S. Federal Reserve Board chairman holding on to higher interest rate worrying about inflation, finally it is through inflation and corresponding wage adjustment that will prevent the imminent recession or if recession occurred it will end as a result of same action" (quote from my e-mail to the Federal Reserve Board dated January 21, 2008. Please note that this message was not edited).

The Federal Reserve Board replied to me, saying, "Your views cannot be simply ignored."

On January 22, 2008, the Federal Reserve Board decided to cut interest rates. Several other rate cuts followed. This was done with the hope that when money was made cheap, it would induce borrowing. However, their target was the entrepreneurs. The entrepreneurs would not invest even if the money was cheap if they could not get what they expected from the consumers.

However, as was expected in a terminal recession, even though money was cheap, the required consumer credit could not flow into the economy to bridge the economic system gap, which ensures that the entrepreneurs get what they expect from consumers out of their expenditure.

Though money was cheap, over-indebted consumers could not borrow, and the lenders were not willing to lend to all the customers, even to those whose credit scores were good, as had been done before.

Because of this very reason, rate cuts did not stop the recession.

Even though the Federal Reserve chairman accepted that the interest rate cuts could result in moderate inflation, still there was no suggestion to increase wages.

In fact, the Federal Reserve Board and the government should have initiated a wage increase bound moderate inflation, which could have aborted the impending recession. Instead, the crisis mounted pressure on the currency, and, as a result, currency devaluation bound inflation, which is negative, began to set in.

I knew without understanding the economic system, as we understood through the theory of economic system gap, that the Federal Reserve would have difficulty in understanding the real crisis. Therefore, I made another attempt to enlighten them on theory.

On January 22, 2008, I wrote to the Federal Reserve Board, saying "This economic crisis is about to change how we will practice economic policy in future. A question that has never raised in economics so far need to be raised now. That question is, can the economic system ever pay consumers an equal or excess amount to the value of consumption? The answer is NO. That means no matter how advance (or rich) the economy is or the volume of employment is, consumers have to borrow as long as capital is continued to accumulate. Then unless the borrowing powers of consumers are revived we cannot stop the recession. The economic system can never pay equal or excess amount to the value of consumption. But if consumers did not buy what is available for consumption, production cannot continue. Therefore consumers have to purchase what is produced for consumption to put the economic system into equilibrium. Then how consumers purchase what is available for consumption having less money? The short answer is 'consumer credit.' This is the fundamental reason that economy cannot thrive without consumer credit. Therefore the need for consumer credit arises from the gap between the value of consumption and consumer income and due to the same reason though consumer credit appears to be personal on the part of individual consumer, but it is not. What does this means? It means in the final analysis it is consumer debt that is capitalized in the hands of entrepreneurs as expanded capital. If there is no consumer credit there is no capital expansion. Accordingly it is clear when consumer credit shrunk a recession is imminent, no matter what the volume of employment is. When the recession set in eventually that will create unemployment. With a huge trade deficit the gap between consumption and consumer income within U.S. should increase needing higher demand for consumer credit for U.S. consumers. When that happen credit cycle cannot sustain for a long time and as this debt can never be paid as a cumulative sum, at a certain point both people as individual consumers and government as institutional consumer should be overwhelmed by debt. We have come to that point. Both people and government cannot borrow as has been done before. When consumers do not borrow or the lenders cannot supply consumer credit, capital expansion does not occur resulting first stagnation and then recession. Supply of credit is not a big issue because we have a good mechanism to do it even is stock market fails completely. The only solution is that we have to revive the borrowing power of consumer. To do that, we need to wipe off part of current consumer debt. As at now the only way to do it is to let the moderate inflation set in and at the same time make an adjustment to the wage structure" (quote from my e-mail to the Federal Reserve Board on January 22, 2008. Please note that this message was not edited for language errors).

The Federal Reserve Board and the government still believed that even though there can be a recessionary effect; it would be similar to the previous short-term recessions that occurred previously.

However, by early February 2008, almost all economists were unanimous that the Federal Reserve Board's rate cuts would not solve the crisis, because the credit market was frozen.

In this situation, the U.S. Congress, which has the Democratic majority, decided to use an old-fashioned strategy with full patronage of the incumbent Republican president.

That strategy was to provide a tax rebate amounting to nearly $170 billion directly to the consumers (i.e., households). They called it a stimulus package. The majority of U.S. households were now to receive free money for consumption.

In fact, the government did not have a budget surplus to provide such a tax rebate. The government needed to borrow that money.

However, it was accepted by the government that consumers in general were in a dire situation and needed extra money outside their legitimate income to sustain the economy even though the employment rate was still high.

Why did the consumers need extra cash outside their legitimate income in order to do their consumption?

That is the question we resolved through the theory of economic system gap. We clearly understood that the economic system can never pay consumers an income equal to the value of consumption.

The value of consumption is what the entrepreneurs expect from the consumers out of their expenditure. If entrepreneurs do not get what they expect from consumers, then they tend to scale down their production or service. That is how the economy goes into a recession.

Therefore, bridging this gap between consumer income, which is less, and the value of consumption is a must. To do that, consumers need extra cash outside their income.

As we saw previously, there are two important tools to provide extra money to consumers. One is private consumer loans such as car loans, credit card facilities, and home loans. The other tool is deficit financing of the government.

All other tools we discussed are either inefficient or not very significant, especially in a crisis.

Now, the 2008 crisis virtually disrupted private consumer borrowing. Even though the Federal Reserve Board brought down interest rates, it did not increase consumer borrowing. Consumers were simply over indebted. It was a clear indication that the consumer credit mechanism was failing; even money was made cheap.

Therefore, the other option was to increase deficit financing. Though the Republican president was talking about budget cuts and exercising fiscal responsibility, the government decided to increase deficit financing.

In normal situations, the government finances certain projects that are important for the society as a whole through deficit financing. This time around, it was unusual. The government immediately decided to provide free cash to the general public—the consumers.

We saw in chapter 2 that deficit financing contributes to bridging the system gap and putting the economic system into equilibrium.

In this case, even though the government did not spent money on specific projects, money was provided directly to the consumers to spend on consumption. Deficit financing is an act of consumption even though it is money spent on so-called capital projects. In this case, it was clearly demonstrated. (We explain this point again in part 2 of this book.)

As the time passes, in mid-2008, again, it was clearly apparent that the crisis was not going to abate. Instead, now the crisis made several bank runs, which I predicted in my letter to the Federal Reserve Board on January 21, 2008. There, I wrote if the debt cancellation process was adopted deliberately through wage adjustments and a moderate inflation process, we would prevent bank runs.

On July 11, 2008, INDYMAC Bank went bankrupt and was taken over by the government. This was the fifth large financial institution that went bankrupt as at July 11, 2008.

Official economists in the Federal Reserve Board perhaps tried to ignore my point of view. Yet, in March, I felt I should do my duty. Again, I wrote to them on March 11, 2008, and they acknowledged my e-mail message.

I wrote the following message.

"Dear Sirs/Madams,

Economic theory rather than data will give you a much understanding about how you should approach this crisis. I guess you are not receptive to that idea. Still I felt I should write to you. Money based economic system whether it is capitalist or socialist or any other behaves in a very unique particular way. To brief it I will put it this way. "We (the consumers) got to borrow to consume to hold on to our jobs and create new ones for our kids. Even to remain stagnant we got to borrow." The need to borrow for consumers arises due to economic system's inability to pay consumers' enough money (income) than the value of consumption offered by the system in a given period. Since though consumer credit appears to be personal on the part of consumers it is not because it is arising from a system gap between consumer income and the value of consumption. The conclusion is, until consumers' borrowing power is revived current recession should be worsening. It will happen for sure. What ever you do in financial market should target to revive consumers borrowing power. But I know your focus is elsewhere. This crisis broke the consumers' ability to borrow and lenders ability to lend of which both are not physical parameters. As such both parameters are maneuverable theoretically for greater good through pro-active policy actions. Consumers' ability to borrow is the only parameter that affects to a recession. Volumes of jobs, innovative ability, productivity etc [sic] do not play any role in preventing a recession. But conventional economic wisdom is yet to understand this (quote from my e-mail to the Federal Reserve Board on March 11, 2008. Please note that this message was not edited).

The Federal Reserve Board thanked me for my views, as usual.

By mid-July 2008, Democratic presidential nominee Barrack Obama started to suggest that the economy might need another stimulus package. That means another increase in deficit financing. The government can borrow money, but private citizens cannot, because still wages are not adjusted and the inflation puts extra constraint on their liquidity.

The crisis hit hard, as this book went to press in September 2008. Now it might be too late to make a wage increase. Yet the fundamental dynamic has to be changed that is, debt to income ratio has to be reduced in general to save the physical economy. There are a number of innovative methods to do it.

All measures taken by the Federal Reserve Board, the government, and what was suggested by senator Obama and McCain were clearly trial-and-error formulas. None of them were guided by theory or suggested solutions were not justified by theory. Until they begin to look at the current issue as an issue of bridging the economic system gap, these authorities will not be able to find a solution other than telling the nation and the world they did what they could.

PART 2
REENGINEERING OF THE
ECONOMIC SYSTEM

PART 2
INTRODUCTION

Here, the word reengineering is used to give the same meaning as it is used in the subject of the business reengineering process (BRP). In 1993, Hammer and Champy defined BPR as "the fundamental rethinking and radical redesign of business processes to achieve dramatic improvements in critical contemporary measures of performance."

I prefer to think that same definition is applicable here, but in the case of the macroeconomic system.

Immediately after the above word is defined, free market economists and advocates might be thinking that I am going to propose a model for a planned economy.

If the words "planned economy" are used for "system planning" rather than planning of individual products, to them our answer should be yes. The reasons for it and the quantitative analyses that are required to reengineer the economic system are outlined in the following chapters.

CHAPTER 5
MARKET MECHANISM VERSUS MONETARY MECHANISM

When the economy hits a crisis, most people believe it is a failure of the market order. Therefore, understanding the role of the market mechanism in the economy is very important.

It is better to start this section with a historical note. In the last week of December 2007, the incumbent U.S. president in his address to the nation said that a recession was unlikely. He cited higher rates of employment, high productivity of the work force, and an innovative ability as reasons to his conclusion. By early January 2008, he accepted that the economy was facing difficulty. Still, he did not want to call it a recession. He called it "a rough patch of the economy."

We now know those variables cited by the president have nothing to do with an economic recession in predicting it or in preventing it. In the theory of economic system gap, we established that an economic recession occurs when the economic system gap is not bridged. This gap is predominantly set to be bridged by the consumer credit mechanism. When the consumer credit mechanism fails, either due to over indebtedness of consumers or lenders' inability to lend, then the economic system gap cannot be bridged. So, the economy should go into a recession. Consumer credit is the single most important variable that should be looked into regarding an economic recession.

Therefore, if the president or, for that matter, the Federal Reserve Board could assure the nation that the consumer credit mechanism will prevail uninterrupted, then we can be sure that a recession is unlikely.

However, when an economic crisis hits, usually unpatriotic entrepreneurs and government corruption are cited as the cause. For example, corporate heads of oil companies were summoned before two Congressional hearings in early 2008. They were made to testify under oath. They were questioned about the net profit of their companies and personal earnings.

Most of the questions were targeted to give the public an impression that the market mechanism is failing. So, government intervention could be demanded to regulate market prices. Simply, fingers were pointed at the wrong cause and demanded the wrong solution.

Yet, something is wrong with the economy. We need a solution. The first thing we have to do is to find the real cause. That is the key to finding a viable solution. So, which is at fault? Is it the market mechanism or the monetary mechanism? This is what we are going to investigate in this chapter.

Micromanagement of the economy by the government is not possible. No government is big enough to micro mange the economy. Regulations cannot be the way to manage economy. That is the truth.

Instead, we need a system to be put in place. In such a system, single government policy decisions would direct resources, including capital, to wherever they need to be allocated. This must be the basis. Any regulatory and administrative measures should only be complementary to that system. Regulations should not be the way of economic management.

What is the best system? Make no mistake; it is the market order. We know the market economy is blamed when there is price instability, inflation, and unemployment. This is entirely wrong. We do not identify the real cause for disturbances in the economy; instead, we attack the market mechanism, which is the best planning tool ever evolved by human kind.

This is not capitalist ideology. For that matter, listen to Trotsky. Leon Trotsky, whom the BBC described as an intellectually arrogant socialist, was absolutely clear on this point.

"Market and credit mechanism serve the cause of socialism better than capitalism." In brief, this is one of the conclusions made by Leon Trotsky in his famous book *The Revolution Betrayed*. We will give you the exact quotes later.

Therefore, the ideological difference between true socialists and capitalists cannot be based on the market order of the economy.

As such, the debate should not be about the enthronement or dethronement of the market mechanism.

However, this debate existed and continues to exist. It is a false debate.

Is there any fundamental reason to choose the market mechanism by both capitalists and intellectually articulate socialists like Trotsky?

If it is a fundamental reason, then it can be scientific and cannot be ideological.

Ricardo, a capitalist economist, one time suggested that a kind of labor certificate should be issued to labor in lieu of cash payment so that there would be no inflation.

Karl Marx rejected this idea entirely and established the essential nature of the market mechanism in the project of economic progress at least as long as money exists.

Karl Marx stated, "The actual sale of commodities for money tests the validity of the expectation that any particular labor expended is indeed social and necessary labor. It is only after sale that the social and necessary character of the labor expended in producing a commodity is guaranteed. The commodity producer produces the commodity on a speculation that the market will validate the social and necessary character of that labor."

He was plainly clear about the role of the market. The consumer has to validate the production by the act of purchasing. By doing that, consumers decide which branches of industry or services should use the scarce resources in the country. It is not certain whether devoted capitalist economists could find a better theoretical reason to explain the role of the market than above. They have to take Marx's word on it, not Ricardo's or any other.

The market mechanism is an essential tool to ensure the use of social resources efficiently in production. That is what Marx explained in the above quote. Even highly sophisticated central planners cannot do it more efficiently than the market mechanism. The market mechanism itself is the best planning tool.

Leon Trotsky recommended this principle be applied in the young Soviet Union under a different frame work of capital ownership. Attacking the price controls of Stalin's regime, he wrote, "The professors forgot to explain how you can estimate real costs if all prices express the will of a bureaucracy and not the amount of socially necessary labor expended. And as to prices, they will serve the cause of socialism better, the more honestly they being [sic] to express the real economic relations of the present day" (Trotsky., *The Revolution Betrayed*).

He further wrote, "Directive prices were less impressive in real life than in the books of scholars." Those are not words from capitalist economists but from a good socialist.

If merchants made good luck out of consumers' tragedy, then Trotsky had a solution. He said, "In reality, for the redistribution of the people's income the government has in its hands such mighty levers as taxes ... the budget and credit mechanism is wholly adequate for a planned distribution of the national income" (Trotsky., *The Revolution Betrayed*). The important point is he did not advocate "administrative" prices in general.

Ironically, Stalin—the ruler after Lenin in the Soviet Union—decided to take Ricardo's word, but awkwardly. In the early 1930s, Soviet Russia issued various cards, such as bread card and an industrial merchandise card. That was the first ever experiment made by a relatively advanced industrialized country to eliminate the market

mechanism and money. In just two years, the whole system failed—
the role of money was accepted and the market exchange of goods
revived but not to the full extent of a free market but with directive
prices.

In view of the above discussion, we converge into one thing, which is
there cannot be a debate in using the market mechanism to produce
consumer goods and services. That is the only efficient way to do it
perhaps until future generations find a better mechanism in the distant
future. This does not mean privatization of all ventures. Immaterial of
the ownership of ventures, prices should reflect the market reality.

Then, what should we really be debating? It is nothing other than how
the market mechanism is best used to create optimum or maximum
wealth and be distributed according to cultural norms of any particular
society.

This debate, in order to be a true debate, must be grounded upon a
scientific base rather than ideological reasons.

Many economists believe economics is not a science. They perhaps
like it to be that way. Can economics be a science? Yes, it can.

In physical sciences, we theorize certain behavioral patterns. For
example, by the first principle of thermodynamics or by the theory of
gravity, scientists explain definite physical phenomena. When tested,
you get the same results repeatedly. So, they become sciences and
scientific theories.

Similarly, we can theorize certain behaviors of the economy. For
example, the money-based economic system behaves in a very unique,
particular way. That behavior means the economic system cannot
pay enough money to the consumers equivalent to the value of
consumption offered by the same system to do the consumption at
any given period of time.

So, this is a principle or unique behavior in money-based exchange
economies. You would get the same results if you tested it in the
United States, Europe, or in any other country, including Sri Lanka.

The said gap exists under normal circumstances in any money-based exchange economy at any level of development. Here "normal circumstances" mean that the country carries no excessive trade surpluses in the long run.

Then, this economic theory is like any other theory in physical sciences, because it explains a particularly unique behavior in the economic system.

However, this gap has to be bridged to put the economic system into equilibrium in order to continue production in accordance with the given physical capacity of production. This is because the value of consumption offered is what the entrepreneurs expect from consumers to recover the capital expended with a surplus for expansion. That is why this gap needs to be filled. We proved this theoretically in part 1 of this book.

Then, which system and under which institutional and political frame work could a healthy gap be created and bridged efficiently, flexibly, and in a sustainable manner to create optimum wealth for any given nation?

This is the true debate that all kinds of politicians, economists, and the population at large should be engaged in. This type of debate is not ideologically based. It has a true scientific basis.

Because of the scientific nature of this debate, at the end of it, beliefs would vanish regarding economic management, and a scientific model would emerge.

However, as we all know, the so-called market economies do not deliver what they promise. They are infected with inflations, recessions, occasional depressions, and unemployment. The true cause for these illnesses is not in the market mechanism but in the money system, without which the market order cannot prevail.

The market process gives the meaning to money and justifies its existence. In turn, the money system provides the infrastructural base for the market to function.

It is the money system that could and should bridge the gap between consumer income and the value of consumption, thereby putting the economic system into equilibrium in order to continue production under the market order. When the money system cannot do the job properly, it surfaces as a problem in the market order.

Since consumers, including private consumers and government consumers, do not get enough money to consume what is offered for consumption under any given period, they need extra money out of the production system. The capitalist economic system has an evolved mechanism to provide this extra sum of money predominantly as credit.

If the gap is filled by credit, then that means we have to borrow to consume to put the economic system into equilibrium; by doing that, we hold on to our jobs and create new ones for our kids.

So, economies have put the credit mechanism in place in the money system's infrastructure to help the market mechanism to take its cause. It is true that the money system is manipulated to satisfy the selfish needs of a few people. Through it, they distort the market mechanism again for their selfish motives. This happens within nation states and internationally too. However, the market order in general is not at fault.

The market order by itself cannot go into a disorder. Only monetary disorder can put the market order into a disorder. This was what happened in the terminal recession of 2008, which we have already discussed in part 1.

In economic management, we have three precise objectives. First, we expect to utilize the country's given physical capacity of production to produce optimum output. Second, we must expand the physical capacity itself to produce more in the future. Third, we need to distribute the distributable output among people according to the norms of society.

How do we achieve the aforementioned three economic objectives? As it goes on in today's politics, managing a country's economy is a matter of good expectations and being uncorrupt. Political parties when in opposition might feel that way. When they come to power, they immediately realize that matters do not work that way. Their 5-year or 10-year plans or more correctly list of ambitious proposals just do not find their way into real life. Why?

The reason is production and distribution cannot be planned in physical quantities. They are to be planned by an abstract quantity known as "money." This is not difficult to understand. For example, let us take the distribution part. You are supposed to consume your daily needs, such as food, and services such as transport or perhaps your home or some other kind of shelter. So, the economic system should provide you a certain amount of money to do that. Your consumption depends on the amount of money you get compared to others.

So, the country produces a certain amount of goods and services for consumption, including arts and music. It has a certain value at current prices, and that is the maximum money that should go to consumers to consume those products and services. If more money is distributed, then inflation occurs.

How is this quantity of money distributed among the members of society? We have three instruments to do it. These instruments are wages, taxes, and consumer credit. We shall discuss these three tools of distribution in detail in the next chapter.

Whatever the case, we achieve distribution of distributable output through the money system. So, it is a job of monetary and fiscal policy. If any political party says that they implement a more equitable distribution, then it is not their plan we need. We need to know how they are going to change the monetary and fiscal policy. More directly, we want to know how they are going to change the wage structure, tax structure, and consumer credit mechanism. This is a matter that falls under the purview of managing the money system.

This is not enough, because on the other side of the equation, we have production. We need a good monetary and fiscal policy on the distribution side that will sustain the production.

In the first place, we need to produce in order to distribute. How do we produce? By the theory of economic system gap , we know that bridging the economic system gap is essential in expanding or continuing production. Again, filling of the gap falls under the purview of managing the money system.

Therefore, both production and distribution are to be planned through the monetary mechanism. Any failure of the market mechanism originates from the failure of the money system. Money is an independently controllable variable, and the money system can be intentionally planned. That is what the Federal Reserve should do. It is this management of the money system that has failed in 2008. This is where correction is needed. To understand this issue, we need to understand the money-based production system fully, which we will discuss in the next chapter.

However, free market production is only a subset (part) of whole production. The other subset is out-of-market production.

Law and order are services produced by the government. The government uses certain resources to produce law and order. These services are not for sale but for the common interest of the society. This is an example of out-of-market production.

So, it is clear that these two subsets represent the full production system. However, there should be balance between these two. That will decide the size of the market production and the size of the out-of-market production or the use of limited social resources by each subset.

Unfortunately for free market champions, this balance is not decided by the market forces. It is a conscious decision that should be made by policy makers. Technically, this decision is made when the government decides its tax revenue and the quantum of deficit financing.

This decision determines the size of free market production. Yet, how should the government make this decision? Is it purely political or are there any economic theories that govern this decision?

The answer to this question is primarily important in reengineering of the economic system. In order to find out the answer, we need to understand the mechanics of the money-based production system. We shall discuss this in the next chapter.

CHAPTER 6
UNDERSTANDING THE FUNDAMENTALS OF A MONEY-BASED PRODUCTION SYSTEM

In a money-based modern economy, production (or use of social resources for production) is basically done by two groups of people. One set of people produces products known as consumer goods/services or products for the use of production of those goods. They use part of the available resources in the country. We can name these producers as enterprises.

Enterprises offer their production to the market; hence, the consuming public validates their use of resources in the process of purchasing. If the consumers do not purchase, then entrepreneurs stop production of that particular item(s). That means he stops using physical resources that are limited on useless products. Therefore, the market plays an important role not only as a place of exchange but also as a point of validation for using social resources by enterprises. In addition, in that sense, the market is a highly efficient and democratic institution, because the consuming public decides what the entrepreneur should produce.

The other group of people organized in an institution called the government uses another part of resources for production. Usually, as a rule, the products of the government, which are known as services, could not be sold for profit. For example, these services could be administration, law and order, research and development, and infrastructure development. These services are produced by the government for the common interest and satisfaction of society.

By any chance, if the government produces a product or service that could be sold for profit, then such an endeavor falls into the category of enterprises. However, it could be government owned. Therefore, irrespective of ownership, we have enterprises on one side and the government on the other side as producers.

Now, the first group of producers (i.e., enterprises) uses money capital to employ the resources for production. They recover the capital invested, usually with a surplus at the point of sale. Hence, the sale is a must for enterprises. Enterprises convert money capital into productive power during the production process and recover the capital through sales proceeds.

The other group of producers, namely the government, does not sell anything they produce. The government also uses money to produce services. Yet, this money is not recovered; therefore, it should be different from the money capital used by enterprises. Primarily, capital has to be recovered through sales if it wants to be capital. Money expended by government is not recovered and, hence, cannot be defined as capital even if part of the money is spent on so-called capital projects.

However, we could only define the money expended by the government as "consumption money" when the origin of government income and the true purpose of government expenditure are considered in a money-based economic system. As the discussion continues, this point will be understood clearly. Yet, interestingly, because of the government's consumption, society would have law and order, administration, research and development, and infrastructure development.

Let us recognize the difference in the type of money both producers employ for production. Enterprises use money capital, while the government uses consumption money for production.

Basically, the money system has to provide money capital to enterprises and consumption money to the government to do the production. If the money system is capable of providing both these producers their "rational" share of money sufficient to employ the available resources almost fully for production, then the society should be satisfied with it, because they have now fully employed the available physical resources.

However, this is not the case in all developing countries and in most of the so-called developed countries too. In fact, much of the global physical productive power is wasted. Let us investigate how the economic system provides each producer their share of money.

Previously, we mentioned that the government's products and services are not sold and hence do not generate proceeds. Then, national revenue/proceeds should be generated only by enterprises. Then, at any given period of accounting, we have total proceeds generated by enterprises—we insist by enterprises only.

The second group of producers, namely the government, does not generate any "real" proceeds.

Total proceeds represent the recovered capital and expanded capital. To understand this point, let us take an example.

An entrepreneur uses $500 to produce something whose value is $590. The capital used up is $500, which is recovered, and $90 is the capital expanded. Therefore, total proceeds consist of those two quantities and should be converted into capital in the next production cycle. Without sale proceeds, capital cannot exist.

Let us also examine what would happen to the capital used up in the current production cycle. In that cycle, capital used up is $500. It is used to buy means of production like raw material, machinery, and employee labor. Out of it, it also pays tax, since tax is a cost of production, and capital reserve is always a quantity after tax.

Raw material cost is an income of another entrepreneur, and he pays labor and other costs of production. As it goes on, it is conceivable that $500 converted into two things down the road, which are labor and tax, if any inefficiency did not tie up the capital flow.

Consumption money is what labor directly gets. They spend it on over consumption. The other portion is tax.

The tax portion goes to the government. It pays its employees, welfare, and pensions, for example, which is all converted into consumption money. Those employees produce services for the common interest. So, tax gets converted into consumption money through the government.

So, it is clear that both wages and taxes are consumption money. Both are allocated from the entrepreneurial activity. These two variables are the most important variables that are required to distribute the distributable output. (The third variable of distribution is the consumer credit, and we will discuss it later.)

Let us investigate this matter further. Now, there are means of consumption to be distributed among producers in a given period. In other words, this is the distributable wealth available. However, we cannot pay/distribute everything to the producers. Out of this, we have to deduct—first to provide for general administration, second for the products/services of the common interest, and third for welfare for those unable to work. We do these deductions through taxes.

After those deductions, the balance is to be distributed among the individual producers. This portion includes net wages of direct producers, including consumption money paid to employers.

In short, we deprive a certain amount to direct producers known as tax. Tax is a part of income deprived to direct producers. However, that money is expended on things of common interest by the government. Karl Marx explained, "What the producer is deprived as an individual will benefit him as a member of society." This is the basis of taxation, and tax is a mechanism to distribute the means of consumption in any given period.

Both wages to direct producers and taxes are consumption money and originate from the cost incurred by enterprises (or proceeds generated and converted as capital by enterprises through market process). *This is the first reason that we define the money expended by government as "consumption money."* However, we know that the consumption money allocated by entrepreneurial activity is not sufficient to do the consumption in full. We know it from the theory of economic system gap, and we will describe that issue later.

Accordingly, as we saw earlier, that capital is produced by enterprises, and now we see consumption money also is made available to society by entrepreneurial activity, not by any other activity (except the amount of consumption money required to fill the economic system gap).

Therefore, it is obvious that there must be an optimum enterprise base in the economic system to generate total proceeds. When the enterprise base is larger, then total proceeds become larger as well as the capital and consumption money that flow from it.

When the enterprise base is bigger, then the use of society's resources by enterprises is bigger. Therefore, the rest of the resources are small and available for government use, which requires less tax. When the enterprise base is smaller, then the taxation will be higher, and the market exchange of goods and services is small, thereby resulting in smaller total proceeds.

Since both capital and consumption money flow from total proceeds, we have to optimize the generation of total proceeds.

In addition, as we learned in chapter 2, enterprise activity creates an economic system gap that must be filled to facilitate generation of the intended total proceeds. Until this gap is filled, the intended total proceeds will not be realized.

In fact, what we want is to realize the intended total proceeds. To realize it, we have to fill the gap between consumer income and consumption, which means the economic system gap. Otherwise, weakening consumption will affect the total demand and the total proceeds, thereby weakening the capital formation.

Therefore, in the final analysis, whatever we do with monetary policy is to try to bridge the economic system gap, knowingly or unknowingly. Now, let us consider the tools available for bridging the economic system gap.

Though we have discussed these tools in chapter 2, it would be appropriate to discuss them here again in detail with the new understanding gained above in part 2 of this book, because those tools constitute an essential part of reengineering of the economic system.

Bridging the Economic System Gap
Provision of Free Money to Consumers

In 1972, the U.S. government sent a check to almost every household in the United States and declared it as a tax rebate. In fact, in that year, the U.S. government did not balance the budget in order to provide a tax rebate. However, consumers got extra money at no cost. That money came outside the production process. However, the point here is that it helped to bridge the gap to a certain extent.

So, one way of bridging the gap is to provide free money by the institution that holds the monopoly to create money. In fact, what is necessary to bridge the gap is extra money, not credit. Provision of free money could be one of them.

In February 2008, the U.S. government repeated this same tax rebate mechanism to provide free money to boost the consumption. The U.S. Congress approved 1 percent of the gross domestic product (GDP), amounting to nearly $170 billion in tax rebates. Ironically, this year, the U.S government also did not balance the budget. So, it has to borrow money to pay for this tax rebate.

Though the tax rebate contributes to bridging the economic system gap temporarily, the justification behind it is totally untrue. Proponents of the tax rebate argued it would boost the consumption and increase the production, and, hence, future tax revenue would be more. From the increased tax revenue in the future, the borrowed money for the tax rebate would be paid off.

We clearly saw that tax is nothing but allocation of consumption money generated by entrepreneurial activity, though the point of collection may differ. At no point, consumption money so allocated is sufficient to do the consumption in full in any given period. Distribution of consumption money between the government and entrepreneurial producer community is not the issue but the inadequacy of the total consumption money.

This gap has been filling primarily by consumer credit. Whatever the cause is, the current (2008) crisis brought that process to a virtual stop. That is why the government has to provide a tax rebate directly to consumers to fill the gap. Therefore, that money has to come outside the production process. Tax is a thing in the domain of entrepreneurial production and distribution. However, deficit financing, which we will explain below, is outside the domain of the entrepreneurial production process. Rather, it is in the domain of the money creation process.

We saw from the theory of the credit cycle that consumers have to be in debt as long as capital continues to accumulate. Deficit financing is a consumption debt, and, together with private consumption debt, that will make the total consumer debt. Both can never be paid as a cumulative sum. Therefore, the argument that this tax rebate could be paid off by future tax income is totally untrue.

However, the tax rebate contributes to bridging the economic system gap to a certain extent.

Provision of Consumer Credit

In theory, what the consumers need is extra money, because, as we saw above, the gap is a creation of the economic system and is no fault of the consumers. However, the society requires responsible consumption by its members. Free extra money does not create that sense of responsibility but credit does.

Credit gives the consumers a sense of responsibility his or her consumption priorities, because products are limited and made with limited resources. Now, the consumers know their liquidity is limited and they will have to pay back whatever credit they take. However, if this is felt as a burden, then the consumers will abstain from taking credit. If that happened, then economic activity would be contracted. Therefore, this sense of responsibility is required only to the extent that it would ensure that the production and consumption would be done without chaos.

Now, remove the credit from the equation. Could any country utilize its physical productive power without consumer credit, which includes deficit financing of the government? The short answer is never. That is what is happening in Germany in this first decade of twenty-first century. Germany records the highest overall unemployment, over 10 percent, and, in eastern Germany, unemployment is nearly 19 percent, even though Germany has a good export program. Consumer lenders have reported that their consumer credit market has been saturated for years, and deficit financing is limited because of European money regulations.

However, though consumer credit consists of private consumer debt and the component of deficit financing, differentiation of both is important. If the government provides free money to consumers through deficit financing, then the consumers' sense of responsibility will be jeopardized. If the government wants to use deficit financing as a tool to bridge the economic system gap, then it do it better by spending money on projects of common interest. Therefore, private consumer credit is a good way of bridging the gap rather than providing free money by the government from time to time.

Deficit Spending

Deficit spending is defined as the money expended by the government to bridge its budget deficit. As we saw above, the government draws its income from the consumption allocation by enterprises by way of taxes. It is not important whether these taxes are deducted directly from enterprises or partly from enterprises and partly from.

Enterprises can pay taxes directly to the government or enterprises can pay that amount to employees and can let the employees pay it to the government. Usually, as in today's practice, both happen. However, this money is consumption money and should be paid to the government to pay for employees who produce services of common interest.

Now, assume the government decided to undertake another project that requires extra money outside its income. So now, there is a deficit in the budget, and extra money expended falls into the category of deficit spending. It can be a construction of a university or any other matter. However, the government has no money to do it. The government undertakes this project and pays a new set of employees during the construction process. To do that, the government needs to bring extra money and, with that money, produce a new category of consumers. This will contribute to bridging the gap.

To have this extra consumption money, the government could either borrow or print new money. The government should not borrow what is intended to be capital or consumption. The government should borrow from the "temporary excess liquidity," which we will define later. When there is no excess liquidity, the government should print money as long as all other tools are not contributing enough to bridge the gap between consumption and consumer income.

So, deficit spending is one way of bridging the economic system gap. Please note here that the second source of government spending is deficit financing. The purpose should be to bridge the economic system gap by creating a new consumer group or by providing extra free money (fake tax rebates) to existing consumers, as we noticed above. Again, deficit financing is for consumption. *This is the second reason we defined the money expended by government as "consumption money".* So, deficit spending certainly contributes to bridging the gap.

We know from our above analysis that the government is a producer but uses consumption money to do its production. Usually, it produces services such as law and order, research and development, and infrastructure. Its revenue is tax that comes from entrepreneurial activity and is used to pay for its employees—a category of consumers.

Now, the consumption money allocated by total entrepreneurial activity is distributed fairly among both employee categories. In addition, both of these categories take out credit to do their consumption. However, wages and consumer credit still might not be sufficient in bridging the economic system gap. Then, only the government can bridge this gap by deficit financing. To do that, the government has to create a new category of employees, and, by doing that, the government produces something of common interest to society (e.g., certain infrastructures).

The government also can enter into forward buying contracts with a certain new set of producers or facilitate that process by providing money originated from deficit financing. Thus, it creates a new set of consumers while ensuring the increase of future national revenue.

Deficit financing is an important not only to bridge the economic system gap but also to increase the national revenue by activating dormant productive power in the country. This is especially true for developing countries. If private entrepreneurs are not willing or are unable to use the existing physical production capacity, then the government should do it through deficit financing with an objective to transform such ventures into enterprise mode in the future that could operate under consumer demand.

However, the rule is the quantum of deficit financing, and private consumer credit should be equal to bridging the economic system gap. If not, excessive deficit financing will create quick inflation.

For example, the U.S. government could provide a certain amount of money to Boeing and Lockheed Martin to invent an efficient propulsion technique. This money is government consumption money financed by either tax or deficit financing. When the solution is found, it is applied in commercial planes bringing new revenue.

The government did the same for agriculture in the early twentieth century. Abundance of agricultural produce today in the U.S. is a direct result of deficit financing in that sector. That is the intelligent way of spending government consumption money, including deficit financing. However, commercial production of any produce in general should not be supported by so-called "administrative prices," which distort the efficient use of social resources.

The government can spend its consumption money on over administration, which will not contribute to any future prosperity even though the economic system gap is filled currently.

The common economic wisdom is that deficit financing should not be done by printing money. This is true only if a mandatory reserve requirement (refer to chapter 1) is constant, because when we treat a mandatory reserve requirement as fixed, printed money increases the supply of credit–money dramatically. We learned that process in chapter 1 under the fractional reserve banking system. However, if we treat the mandatory reserve requirement as a variable, then we can use it with the amount of printed money to fill the economic system gap efficiently. Printed money is debt-free money for the government.

If money is printed for deficit spending, then the mandatory reserve requirement has to increase by a certain percentage to stabilize the credit and money supply. However, we cannot arbitrarily decide the amount of deficit financing. It is the balance amount of money needed to fill the economic system gap when other tools are not sufficient. Any arbitrary determination of over deficit and financing it with printed or even credit–money will create quick inflation.

Whatever the case, we now know that deficit financing will bridge the economic system gap.

Investment of Self-Expanded Capital and Producer Credit

In the recovery of capital through total proceeds, we noticed above that part is allocated for expansion. When this is invested, a new group (new employees and their dependents) will become consumers. That contributes to bridging the gap in the period that is being invested.

In addition, credit is issued to new producers of both kinds, namely consumer goods producers and higher-order goods producers. Higher-order goods producers produce goods to be utilized by consumer goods producers. During this process, they convert part of the capital advanced into consumption money by paying employees. It creates a new group of active consumers, and their income, including possible credit, could contribute to bridging the gap.

This action is very similar to the government's deficit spending. However, in this case, when the production of new enterprises comes into the market in the future, it will widen the gap. However, this process should continue until the work force is fully employed.

So, investment is another way of bridging the gap today, but it creates a greater gap tomorrow, since all investments are to be recovered, in the final analysis, through consumer sales. Therefore, investments of self-expanded capital and investments made with producer credit could not be strictly regarded as a tool to bridging the economic system gap.

Making Money from Money for Consumption (Stock Market)

Mr. Allen Greenspan, the former U.S. Federal Reserve chairman, once said that out of each $4 invested in the stock market, $1 goes into consumption. (The Federal Reserve System is the U.S. version of the Central Bank.) When the stock prices increase, investors sell their stocks. In the process, they make some gains, and part of it is utilized for consumption. Let us assume we are buying a car for personal use. However, it is not certain whether Greenspan meant this type of consumption or consumptions made through credit instruments.

If he meant by the above statement consumptions made through (nonbank centered) credit instruments extended by financial markets, then we can disregard it here, because it falls under the category of consumer credit, and we have already discussed it. However, if he meant consumption made through the so-called capital gain by buying and selling stocks, then that is what we will consider here.

In the stock market, you make money out of money through a bidding process but do not produce any service or product to satisfy any human need.

Yet, the stock market is a mechanism to provide money for consumption to bridge the gap. However, as we shall see later, this is a game that could be played by excess liquidity owners, which is not available for the majority of the consuming community and, hence, is not considered an efficient and effective tool.

Credit Card

In developed countries, one of the important consumer credit tools is the credit card. This is not a new tool, but it falls into the category of consumer credit.

Other Tools

Perhaps, readers might find novel tools of bridging the gap. It might be helpful to investigate them. Interest income could be one of them, but those interests finally add up to the cost of goods, making no real impact in bridging the gap.

Now, as we saw above, in a money-based economy, many tools have evolved to bridge the gap between the consumption and the consumer income, thereby generating maximum total proceeds. This is important, because new capital is formed and realized only if the intended total proceeds are made.

We also realized that the only effective and efficient tool to bridging the economic system gap is consumer credit. Perhaps, the other best option is deficit financing. Even if there are numerous tools to bridge the gap, consumer credit plays a major role. The objective of filling the economic system gap is to facilitate capital accumulation, because productive capital creates wealth.

If the economy responds well, this process should not create any problem in the economic system. The process we are referring to is the creation of the economic system gap and filling it primarily by credit and use of expanded capital to expand production. As long as the credit cycle is managed, we should not have any problem.

The managing of credit means it should be able to pay yesterday's credit with today's increased income and increased credit.

Unfortunately, this process is not very smooth because of the inherent contradiction. We explained the reasons in chapter 2. As a result of filling the economic system gap, we face two definite problems. One is the inability to sustain the consumer credit cycle after a certain period of time as a result of the accumulated consumer debt. As a result, consumers cannot keep on borrowing without defaulting significantly.

Second, because of the same reason of filling the economic system gap by consumer credit, which now includes deficit financing, it creates excess liquidity in the system, thereby threatening inflation.

Both these problems have to be addressed to reengineer the economic system.

From the theory of the credit cycle, we noticed that at the end of the credit cycle, part of the consumer debt must be canceled to revive the borrowing power of consumers to go for another cycle. General cancellation of debt through wage increase bound moderate inflation would be a better way to do it. In a certain way, it is also a method to remove excess liquidity.

Therefore, both above issues are investigated together in the following discussion.

Excess Liquidity

The above understanding makes our problem clear. We must expand the credit supply up to a point where available physical resources are utilized for production. This is a far more important objective than so-called monetary stability. To prevent inflation, we need to remove excess liquidity. Then, we will have the monetary stability again.

As we know, we generate total proceeds from enterprising activity. We allocate a certain amount to be capital. However, assume if we reserve more for capital but it is not immediately utilized, then that portion cannot be defined as capital, because money becomes productive capital only during the purchasing of factors of production. This amount is in excess. This extra money is exactly what we defined as excess liquidity, which is the money that is not required as capital or consumption money at the current price level.

Now, in modern money-based economies, we saw above that numerous tools have evolved to bridge the gap. However, capitalism has not produced good innovative tools to remove excess liquidity. Instead, they use unnecessarily complicated and inefficient tools, and, moreover, they use caution against the supply of money in controlling inflation, thereby sacrificing the good part of productive power within nation states and globally.

Caution against money supply is the theory advocated by international financial institutions, especially for developing countries. So, developing countries are destined to carry on with poverty and unemployment, until the trickledown theory works for them—perhaps in decades down the road, even though they have the physical capacity of production now.

Removal of excess liquidity is important to allow the maximum supply of credit (and money) in order to allow the formation of maximum capital without trigging inflation. Today's capitalism is incapable of producing maximum productive capital.

Removal of Excess Liquidity

Use of available physical resources for production is a social objective, and achieving that objective requires the removal of excess liquidity. Then, removal of excess liquidity becomes an objective of the government.

Tools Available for Removing Excess
Liquidity in Today's Capitalism

(1) Stock Market

As we noticed above, we generate total proceeds from enterprising activity. We allocate a certain amount to be capital. However, assume if we reserve more for capital but it is not immediately utilized, then that portion cannot be defined as capital, because money becomes capital only during the purchasing of factors of production. This amount is in excess. This extra money is exactly what we defined as excess liquidity.

Who owns this excess liquidity? Essentially, capital owners own this. This excess liquidity is gradually building up in each accounting cycle.

Now, assume we created an institute to register the real capital invested by enterprises or part of the capital of some of those enterprises. This capital is limited. Now, let the holders of excess liquidity bid for the capital listed. So, the value rises as a result of bidding. However, as far as it continues, it does not create any inflation in consumables, since that money is tied up in a bidding process outside the production cycle. As this process continues, part of the profit earned from pure bidding turns into consumption money. This institution is called the stock market.

Accordingly, we see that a well-developed stock market for a certain period can be a good absorber of excess liquidity in the absence of another innovative tool. Value of the listed shares represents the value of real capital, and so-called market capitalization to a certain extent indicates the level of absorption of excess liquidity. Market capitalization is several times higher than the capital listed. Accordingly, the stock market plays a bigger role as an excess liquidity absorber rather than its role of raising equity capital for new investments.

However, without assessing the comparative advantages in today's stock market, we can say—apart from being instrumental in raising equity capital—it is important in two counts (i.e., to provide extra consumption money to bridge the economic system gap and to absorb excess liquidity). This later role is far more important.

However, today's stock market is not simply a stock market. It is a credit market too. Why do the economic systems need a credit market when the fractional reserve banking system can take care of the credit requirement of the society along with the government? To understand this issue, we have to understand the evolution process of financial markets.

As we saw above, excess liquidity is an uncapitalized sum of money in the hands of entrepreneurs. So, they own it.

We also saw above that excess liquidity is pushing up the prices of stocks. If they go up or down, there is no big effect on the economy if the credit mechanism is not taken up by the stock market.

If I have to present an analogue, I will take the example of a horse race. There are several factors that are affecting the horses that actually run. Those are real physical factors like strength, body mass, and training. Now, outside the ring, speculators are bidding for the winner. What is happening in the bidding process has no impact on the horses or on the jockeys who run the race. The stock market at this stage (that means without being instrumental to supply credit) is similar to this bidding process happening outside the ring.

Seeing the stock prices going up, saving institutions such as insurance companies and pension funds start their bidding too, in turn pushing the prices up further.

Average consumers also are attracted by seeing the upward trend of the stock market, but they do not have money to buy stocks. Our fractional reserve bankers who can create any amount of money out of nothing come to their rescue. Bankers offer credit to purchasers of stocks up to the value of 65 percent of the market price. So, they take loans and join the stock market. Then, prices of stocks go up once again.

Foreign investors also join to make quick money.

Funds invested in buying stocks cannot stay along. They come into the banking system. The system now possesses massive excess liquidity.

Entrepreneurial excess liquidity and fractional reserve banking are a lethal combination if abused. It can create a massive credit boom. It lends domestically, internationally, and to poor countries through the World Bank.

On the other side of the story, consumers accumulate debt on a continuous basis. Credits are taken to pay old debt. Eventually, providing consumer credit becomes riskier. However, financiers have a solution. Banks are governed by a certain set of rules. They cannot charge subprime rates. So, they convert the stock market into a credit market.

Usually, lenders who take higher risks in lending charge more fees for their financial instrument to consumer clients. These institutions now get financed from financial markets. They become lenders to consumer clients (usually producer investors do not borrow from them). Now the so-called stock market begins to play the role of extending credit to consumers, which was supposed to be done by the banking system. However, these consumer loans are disastrous to consumers. These loans are structured in a way that they become expensive as time passes. Lenders assume that consumer income rises in order to service loans when loans become expensive. That assumption is not realistic when the monetary policy targets the inflation. As this process continues, the credit cycle becomes unsustainable quickly, because cumulative consumer debt-to-income ratios become higher.

Realizing the threat of defaulting of loans, stock market financiers then withhold the credit supply. The credit market has been filling the economic system gap, and when it is disrupted, the economic system gap is not filled. When the economic system gap is not filled, the entrepreneurs do not get what they expect from the consumers out of their expenditure; as a result, investments and production are discouraged, and a recession begins to set in.

It is not the plunging stock prices that cause the recession; instead, it is the crunching of consumer credit initially by financiers themselves that cause the recession. In fact, if the stock market's ability to extend consumer credit is removed, then the stock market would never seriously affect the physical economy.

(2) Real Estate Market

Perhaps, someone would prefer to think the real estate market absorbs excess liquidity. They argue that asset bubbles soak up the excess liquidity.

Assets are in general of two kinds known as stocks and properties and appear to absorb excess liquidity, thereby creating inflation in those areas but preventing the inflation from spilling into regular day-to-day consumables. We discussed the role of stocks above in absorbing excess liquidity.

Any presence of excess liquidity should create inflation. So, they happen in so-called investment domains, avoiding in general inflation.

However, there is a sharp distinction between stock bubbles and property bubbles. Any inflation in properties affects consumption. If a person wants to buy a house in which to live, then financiers call it an asset, which it is not. It is consumption. You need to buy a loan to do that consumption. It is almost like your car, but it is more durable than your car. If you buy a house to rent out, then that is again a house, but it is an asset.

Now, assume that real estate prices are in an upward trend. That means there is inflation in the real estate market. So, you are required to make a higher investment now to buy the house from which you intend to make an income.

So, it becomes necessary that you have to increase the rent to recover your investment, thereby translating that inflation into the consumption of the renter.

Property inflation contributes to the increase of consumer expenditure, thereby making the consumer credit cycle unsustainable. Therefore, though property assets absorb excess liquidity, it should be reflected in production and consumption of those assets and, therefore, not an instrument to absorb excess liquidity.

However, stocks (sometimes government debt instruments are called stocks, but they are not considered stocks here), which mean corporate shares, really absorb excess liquidity (temporarily) without any impact on production and consumption. They are in the domain of the monetary infrastructure.

In addition, some economists believe government bonds are issued not to borrow but to control the money supply to prevent inflation by removing excesses. It is shear ignorance.

(3) Rates of Interest and Reserve Rate

One of my colleagues asked why we cannot treat the rate of interest as a tool of removing excess liquidity. What is important is to maintain an efficient consumer credit mechanism to bridge the economic system. When that happens, entrepreneurs get what they expect from consumers out of their expenditure, and the economy should be in good shape.

When interest rates increase, it contracts the money supply. Such rate increases should not affect the credit flow into consumers or households. However, if it affects the consumer credit mechanism, then easily such an action would produce negative results.

Targeting the rate of interest was the preferred policy tool by most central bankers and theorists, at least in the past couple of decades, to control inflation.

Alan S. Blinder, the renowned Princeton University professor and former vice chairman of the Federal Reserve Board, said, "Interest targeting won by default in the United States and elsewhere" (Blinder 1998).

The economic crisis of 2008 brought this proud claim to disrepute. The Federal Reserve Bank observed an inflationary trend and increased the rate of interest to control inflation in 2006.

Unlike previous times, this time, when the Federal Reserve Board increased interest rates to control inflation, the massive U.S. economy began to slip into a recession.

The Federal Reserve Board abandoned the targeting of interest rates amidst inflation. In fact, the Federal Reserve Board brought down rates during inflation in late 2007 and early 2008. However, these actions could not revive the badly damaged consumer credit mechanism. The policy that worked for a certain period of time failed this time around. That policy now failed in the United States and is failing elsewhere.

We choose our policies based on a trial-and-error basis and not on good theory. That is what Professor Blinder meant when he said that targeting the rate of interest won by default.

However, India, which is now becoming a reasonably fast-growing economy, decided to target the mandatory reserve requirement to control inflation instead of increasing the rate of interest. By doing that, India might have expected to control domestically responsible inflation while keeping relatively low rates of interests without overburdening the consumer and producer entrepreneur. However, India should ensure that primarily the consumer credit cum the government deficit financing can satisfactorily bridge the economic system gap. That is what is important in preventing the economy from slipping into a recession while controlling inflation.

Accordingly, the rate of interest is not a good tool to remove excess liquidity even though it might be useful in the short term to control money in circulation together with the mandatory reserve rate. However, it is important to ensure the required amount of credit flows into the economy to bridge the economic system gap while controlling money in circulation.

(4) Moderate Inflation and Corresponding Wage Adjustments as a Tool to Remove Excess Liquidity

Still, we have not recognized the requirement of creating consumer credit and removing excess liquidity positively. Had we known the importance of removing excess liquidity, we could have found new instruments to do it. In the event, especially developing countries could have activated a powerful consumer credit cycle required for economic growth while controlling the inflation.

A well-managed credit cycle could have a long life period. However, since consumer credit as a collective sum can never be paid, credit continues to accumulate. However, surely over time, it will bring negative pressure on consumers, which could reduce consumer spending. We learned about it earlier in chapter 2.

Once the present credit cycle puts negative pressure on consumers, a new cycle should start before the economy collapses.

However, toward the end of the credit cycle, consumers cannot borrow as a result of overwhelmed debt. In order to revive their borrowing power once again, we have to cancel part of their debt safely. It is an economic necessity. The best way I can think of is to allow moderate inflation to set in, and adjust the wage structure to suite it.

Increased wages do not bring any real additional buying power to consumers, because inflation has offset it. However, as a result of this process, even though consumers pay numerically their loan premiums, their debt is partially canceled.

Perhaps, an economy can perform this act in suitable time periods without waiting for the end of a credit cycle.

In addition, this can be the most important tool for partial cancellation of consumer debt to revive the borrowing power of consumers, which is essential to ensure that the entrepreneurs get what they expect from consumers out of their expenditure, thereby bridging the economic system gap.

(5) Other Tools for Removing Excess Liquidity

These tools have yet to be uncovered in the process of quantitative analysis in applying this theory into the economy. They might vary from country to country.

Excess liquidity is a byproduct in the economy resulting from filling the economic system gap predominantly by consumer credit. However, excess liquidity is owned by enterprises. It is not real capital reserve. So, there should not be any hard feelings if that excess is removed and destroyed from the money system to have a greater stability in the economy, in which everybody benefits.

So, in view of the above analysis, we now know maintaining a healthy economic system gap, filling it by consumer credit, and removing excess liquidity constitute the essential elements of reengineering the economic system to have an efficient economy.

However, we have to start with total proceeds or revenue, since both main sources of consumption money and money capital are flowing from it.

Increasing the Volume of Total Proceeds and Determining the Size of the Government

As we noticed above, it is required to start with potential total proceeds in reorganizing the economy. We have to increase total proceeds. To do that, we have to expand the market exchange of products and services. As we shall see later, a new kind of monetary policy will have to be put in place to ensure that money will not set any limit for production, but physical capacity or human needs will set the limit for production.

To increase total proceeds, we have to start with the government. If the government is involved in using much of the resources for production as it is now, it must put most of those endeavors in enterprising mode.

Either the government has to privatize those production and service units or they must convert them into government-owned enterprises if efficiency could be maintained and operate under consumer demand. That will increase the volume of total proceeds.

Through privatization of government ventures, nobody will be deprived in accessing the products or services that were produced by the government earlier, because monetary and fiscal policy (defined below) is set to increase the consumer liquidity. However, by putting the production and service units in enterprising mode, it increases the total proceeds that allocate capital for enterprises and money for consumption while ensuring the efficient use of social resources. (We discussed the essential nature of market order in the economy in chapter 5.)

For an example, let us assume a utility company formerly run by the government to provide electricity. So, the government had to collect taxes to meet its expenses, meaning the government deprived a certain group of producers of their income. When the institution is converted into an enterprising mode, the government does not need to collect taxes to pay for it, meaning producers income will go up. So, they have money to pay for whatever services they buy from the utility company. When it is operated under consumer demand, efficiency would be better and should reflect the actual prices. Administrative prices are always negative, because it restricts the production of capital.

If a certain group still cannot afford to buy the services, then the government can use part of government consumption money to provide cash subsidy. There is nothing wrong in doing that. That is the way to distribute social produce while allowing capital accumulation.

People might think the private utility company might increase tariff and make a huge profit. As long as this profit is not transformed into excess liquidity, it is good for the society, because that profit is converted into productive capital; in turn, it should generate more electricity.

Wage rates of employees are another area that needed reform and understanding. Wage rates are not an issue as long as credit flow increases the buying power of workers, which is required to bridge the economic system gap and generate total proceeds, and as long as entrepreneurs do not carry any long-term excess liquidity.

Entrepreneurs' luxurious consumption is not a big deal, because that consumption contributes to generating total proceeds. If it is a concern, then it can easily be countered with fiscal policy (through taxes).

During the early stages of development, a country might need to allow for speedier capital expansion. That means we will have to have a bigger system gap. Employees might understand this as exploitation of their labor. However, it is not as long as self-expanded capital is invested.

However, if it is not invested, it will convert into excess liquidity, and part of it might be utilized for extreme luxurious consumption by capital owners. Definitely, this has a shadow of exploitation and could be remedied willingly, as both employers and employees now know total proceeds are generated not only from their capital alone but also from consumer credit expansion, later being originated from the government policy on social consensus.

As we saw above, wages, government taxes, and consumer credits are the tools of distribution. In addition, government consumption should be more productive oriented (i.e., it must create services for the common satisfaction of the society through its consumption). Over administration is a waste of money, but we could have a bigger government producing real services, including scientific research. The size of the government would shrink once the enterprise base is expanded.

Furthermore, the government should not tax what is intended to be capital. It might appear as a tax concession to enterprises, but surely people would understand the purpose of it once they see the benefits of capital being invested. However, the government should not hesitate to tax excess liquidity beyond a certain limit if it is necessary. The purpose of such a tax is to remove excess liquidity from the system.

Once the economic system is set up (or reformed), as explained above, it has enormous power to be flexible to adjust to any situation just by dictating the policy. One such single policy could activate the whole consumer and entrepreneurial community to do what is required by the society in which they themselves are the members. This is the key to organizing a fast-growing sustainable and people-friendly economy. This arrangement is the base. Any favorable institutional and legal arrangement will only be supportive and complementary.

Monetary Policy

In view of the above, monetary policy is defined as policies that are required to create a healthy economic system gap and to bridge it by good tools and policies required to remove excess liquidity to manage inflation.

Fiscal Policy

Fiscal policies are defined as policies that require distribution of the consumable production, arising from the entrepreneurial activity, among members of society and policies that would require resources be directed to areas for future growth where the market cannot foresee but science could.

Those requirements define the objective function of the Central Bank.

Accordingly, failure to use the available physical productive power for production arises from the failure of monetary policy, while failure of fair distribution and inability to direct resources for future growth arises from a failed fiscal policy.

The current theory of central banking is totally inadequate in addressing the real needs of the economic system. Federal Reserve Chairman Ben S. Bernanke said, "Monetary policy (that is, the management of the short-term interest rate) is the Fed's best tool for pursuing our macroeconomic objectives, namely to promote maximum sustainable employment and price stability" (refer to annexure 1 for Bernanke's testimony on January 17, 2008 at the Congressional budget committee).

The economic crisis of 2008 demonstrated the inadequacy of such a narrow scope for monetary policy in achieving our macroeconomic objectives. In fact, in his above testimony, Federal Reserve chairman Bernanke himself admitted it.

He said: "A number of analysts have raised the possibility that fiscal policy actions might usefully complement monetary policy in supporting economic growth over the next year or so. I agree that fiscal action could be helpful in principle, as fiscal and monetary stimulus together may provide broader support for the economy than monetary policy actions alone" (refer to annexure 1 for the complete testimony).

So, why do not both monetary and fiscal policies come under the purview of the central bank and take the full responsibility, leaving the policy makers to decide on the nation's overall economic direction?

For an example, let us assume we increased taxes and balanced the budget. Then, lending for private consumers has to be softened in order to facilitate the filling of the system gap. Similarly, if we cut taxes, then deficit spending might go up. Therefore, now it is required that the amount of deficit spending and private consumer credit should only be sufficient to fill the economic system gap, and, as a result, relatively tighter private consumer lending might be required.

Accordingly, the debate about the cutting or increasing of taxes has become meaningless political rhetoric. What is important is to maintain a healthy economic system gap and use effective tools to bridge it in a sustainable manner.

This is a job that can be done only by managing the nation's money system as a whole. Both monetary policy and fiscal policy constitute an integral part of it. Therefore, all of these should be the job of the Central Bank. As such, the Central Bank should cease to be privately owned. It must be independent, perhaps like judiciary. In other words, the Central Bank should be the fourth independent branch of government.

With good mathematical modeling, those monetary and fiscal policies could be proactively determined, because all variables discussed above are calculable or estimable. Such practice would generate the maximum productive capital that is exactly sufficient to put the physical productive power into use at any given time, and distribute the distributable produce as the community wants it.

Chapter 7
Conclusive Remarks

We have three precise objectives regarding economics. Those objectives are to (1) use the available physical production capacity for the production of products for the well-being of human kind, (2) enhance the physical productive potential itself in areas where human kind needs it, and (3) distribute the distributable wealth (or output) according to the norms of the society.

We need a mechanism to achieve above the objectives. We theoretically established that the mechanism has to be an enterprise-based system. However, none of the above objectives can be achieved without a plan. Planning of the above objectives is not possible in physical quantities. Planning has to be done by an abstract quantity known as "money."

Modern money is an independently controllable variable. We can produce any amount of it without much problem.

However, creation of money in the right quantities and distribution of it among various economic agents to achieve the above economic objectives have failed so far. In other words, the monetary mechanism is flawed.

It is a failure that results from wrong economic analysis and theory. So far, none of the theorists have raised the question we raised at the beginning of our analysis in this book.

That question is as follows. Can the economic system ever pay the consumers an exceeding or equal amount to the value of consumption under normal circumstances?

Resolving this question will change the whole approach to monetary and fiscal policy. Thus, the production, distribution, and destruction of money will be able to be grounded upon scientific basis for the first time through which we could achieve the said economic objectives.

This does not mean that the trial-and-error methods that have worked so far did not bring any prosperity. Certainly, they did. However, 45 million Americans still run the risk of being without health care, and another good number of people are scared of losing employment and their livelihood during recessions, which occur from time to time.

Globally, nearly 2 billion men, women, and children go to sleep at night without food. One single food crisis puts another 850 million people into hunger in the latter part of the first decade of twenty-first century.

All these happen in spite of having great physical productive potential or having a greater ability to increase physical productive potential thanks to the hard work of scientists. Sometimes, even scientists' potential is constrained by the flawed money system.

However, without changing the money system, we will not achieve the said economic objectives fully.

Millennium challenge goals of the United Nations, charitable donations to the developing world, and "fake" tax rebates in the United States during recessions only serve the purpose of doing damage control. We need to have a better economic methodology to achieve our economic objectives.

The necessary qualitative analysis has been presented in this book. We established through our analysis that maintaining a healthy economic system gap, filling it primarily by consumer credit (which now includes deficit spending), and removing excess liquidity constitute the essential elements of reengineering the economic system to have an efficient economy.

Accordingly, the scope of central banking has to be broadened to incorporate these economic system requirements.

Quantitative analysis has to be followed for application of the theory.

ANNEXURE 1

Chairman Ben S. Bernanke

The economic outlook

**Before the Committee on the Budget,
U.S. House of Representatives**

January 17, 2008

Chairman Spratt, Representative Ryan, and other members of the Committee, I am pleased to be here to offer my views on the near-term economic outlook and related issues.

Developments in Financial Markets

Since late last summer, financial markets in the United States and in a number of other industrialized countries have been under considerable strain. Heightened investor concerns about the credit quality of mortgages, especially subprime mortgages with adjustable interest rates, triggered the financial turmoil. Notably, as the rising rate of delinquencies of subprime mortgages threatened to impose losses on holders of even highly rated securities, investors were led to question the reliability of the credit ratings for a range of financial products, including structured credit products and various special-purpose vehicles. As investors lost confidence in their ability to value complex financial products, they became increasingly unwilling to hold such instruments. As a result, flows of credit through these vehicles have contracted significantly.

As these problems multiplied, money center banks and other large financial institutions, which in many cases had served as sponsors of these financial products, came under increasing pressure to take the assets of the off-balance-sheet vehicles onto their own balance sheets. Bank balance sheets were swelled further by holdings of nonconforming mortgages, leveraged loans, and other credits that the banks had extended but for which well-functioning secondary markets no longer existed. Even as their balance sheets expanded, banks began to report large losses, reflecting marked declines in the market prices of mortgages and other assets. Thus, banks too became subject to valuation uncertainty, as could be seen in the sharp movements in their share prices and in other market indicators such as quotes on credit default swaps. The combination of larger balance sheets and unexpected losses prompted banks to become protective of their liquidity and balance sheet capacity and thus to become less willing to provide funding to other market participants, including other banks. Banks have also evidently become more restrictive in their lending to firms and households. More-expensive and less-available credit seems likely to impose a measure of restraint on economic growth.

The Outlook for the Real Economy

To date, the largest effects of the financial turmoil appear to have been on the housing market, which, as you know, has deteriorated significantly over the past two years or so. The virtual shutdown of the subprime mortgage market and a widening of spreads on jumbo mortgage loans have further reduced the demand for housing, while foreclosures are adding to the already-elevated inventory of unsold homes. New home sales and housing starts have both fallen by about half from their respective peaks. The number of homes in inventory has begun to edge down, but at the current sales pace the months' supply of new homes has continued to climb, and home prices are falling in many parts of the country. The slowing in residential construction, which subtracted about 1 percentage point from the growth rate of real gross domestic product in the third quarter of 2007, likely curtailed growth even more in the fourth quarter, and it may continue to be a drag on growth for a good part of this year as well.

Recently, incoming information has suggested that the baseline outlook for real activity in 2008 has worsened and that the downside risks to growth have become more pronounced. In particular, a number of factors, including continuing increases in energy prices, lower equity prices, and softening home values, seem likely to weigh on consumer spending as we move into 2008. Consumer spending also depends importantly on the state of the labor market, as wages and salaries are the primary source of income for most households. Labor market conditions in December were disappointing; the unemployment rate increased 0.3 percentage point, to 5.0 percent from 4.7 percent in November, and private payroll employment declined. Employment in residential construction posted another substantial reduction, and employment in manufacturing and retail trade also decreased significantly. Employment in services continued to grow, but at a slower pace in December than in earlier months. It would be a mistake to read too much into one month's data. However, developments in the labor market will bear close attention.

In the business sector, investment in equipment and software appears to have been sluggish in the fourth quarter, while nonresidential construction grew briskly. In light of the softening in economic activity and the adverse developments in credit markets, growth in both types of investment spending seems likely to slow in coming months. Outside the United States, however, economic activity in our major trading partners has continued to expand vigorously. U.S. exports will likely continue to grow at a healthy pace in coming quarters, providing some impetus to the domestic economy.

Financial conditions continue to pose a downside risk to the outlook. Market participants still express considerable uncertainty about the appropriate valuation of complex financial assets and about the extent of additional losses that may be disclosed in the future. On the whole, despite improvements in some areas, the financial situation remains fragile, and many funding markets remain impaired. Adverse economic or financial news thus has the potential to increase financial strains and to lead to further constraints on the supply of credit to households and businesses.

Even as the outlook for real activity has weakened, some important developments have occurred on the inflation front. Most notably, the same increase in oil prices that may be a negative influence on growth is also lifting overall consumer prices. Last year, food prices also increased exceptionally rapidly by recent standards, further boosting overall consumer price inflation. The most recent reading on overall personal consumption expenditure inflation showed that prices in November were 3.6 percent higher than they were a year earlier. Core price inflation (which excludes prices of food and energy) has stepped up recently as well, with November prices up almost 2-1/4 percent from a year earlier. Part of this rise may reflect pass-through of energy costs to the prices of core consumer goods and services, as well as the effects of the depreciation of the dollar on import prices, although some other prices--such as those for some medical and financial services--have also accelerated lately.

Thus far, the public's expectations of future inflation appear to have remained reasonably well anchored, and pressures on resource utilization have diminished a bit. Further, futures markets suggest that food and energy prices will decelerate over the coming year. Given these factors, overall and core inflation should moderate this year and next, so long as the public's confidence in the Federal Reserve's commitment to price stability is unshaken. However, any tendency of inflation expectations to become unmoored or for the Fed's inflation-fighting credibility to be eroded could greatly complicate the task of sustaining price stability and reduce the central bank's policy flexibility to counter shortfalls in growth in the future. Accordingly, in the months ahead we will be closely monitoring the inflation situation, particularly inflation expectations.

Monetary Policy Response

The Federal Reserve has taken a number of steps to help markets return to more orderly functioning and to foster its economic objectives of maximum sustainable employment and price stability. Broadly, the Federal Reserve's response has followed two tracks: efforts to improve market liquidity and functioning and the pursuit of our macroeconomic objectives through monetary policy.

To help address the significant strains in short-term money markets, the Federal Reserve has taken a range of steps. Notably, on August 17, the Federal Reserve Board cut the discount rate—the rate at which it lends directly to banks—by 50 basis points, or 1/2 percentage point, and it has since maintained the spread between the federal funds rate and the discount rate at 50 basis points, rather than the customary 100 basis points. In addition, the Federal Reserve recently unveiled a term auction facility, or TAF, through which pre-specified amounts of discount window credit can be auctioned to eligible borrowers. The goal of the TAF is to reduce the incentive for banks to hoard cash and increase their willingness to provide credit to households and firms. In December, the Fed successfully auctioned $40 billion through this facility. And, as part of a coordinated operation, the European Central Bank and the Swiss National Bank lent an additional $24 billion to banks in their respective jurisdictions. This month, the Federal Reserve is auctioning $60 billion in twenty-eight-day credit through the TAF, to be spread across two auctions. TAF auctions will continue as long as necessary to address elevated pressures in short-term funding markets, and we will continue to work closely and cooperatively with other central banks to address market strains that could hamper the achievement of our broader economic objectives.

Although the TAF and other liquidity-related actions appear to have had some positive effects, such measures alone cannot fully address fundamental concerns about credit quality and valuation, nor do these actions relax the balance sheet constraints on financial institutions. Hence, they alone cannot eliminate the financial restraints affecting the broader economy. Monetary policy (that is, the management of the short-term interest rate) is the Fed's best tool for pursuing our macroeconomic objectives, namely to promote maximum sustainable employment and price stability.

Monetary policy has responded proactively to evolving conditions. As you know, the Federal Open Market Committee (FOMC) cut its target for the federal funds rate by 50 basis points at its September meeting and by 25 basis points each at the October and December meetings. In total, therefore, we have brought the federal funds rate down by 1 percentage point from its level just before the financial strains emerged. The Federal Reserve took these actions to help offset the restraint imposed by the tightening of credit conditions and the weakening of the housing market. However, in light of recent changes in the outlook for and the risks to growth, additional policy easing may well be necessary. The FOMC will, of course, be carefully evaluating incoming information bearing on the economic outlook. Based on that evaluation, and consistent with our dual mandate, we stand ready to take substantive additional action as needed to support growth and to provide adequate insurance against downside risks.

Financial and economic conditions can change quickly. Consequently, the FOMC must remain exceptionally alert and flexible, prepared to act in a decisive and timely manner and, in particular, to counter any adverse dynamics that might threaten economic or financial stability.

A number of analysts have raised the possibility that fiscal policy actions might usefully complement monetary policy in supporting economic growth over the next year or so. I agree that fiscal action could be helpful in principle, as fiscal and monetary stimulus together may provide broader support for the economy than monetary policy actions alone. But the design and implementation of the fiscal program are critically important. A fiscal initiative at this juncture could prove quite counterproductive, if (for example) it provided economic stimulus at the wrong time or compromised fiscal discipline in the longer term.

To be useful, a fiscal stimulus package should be implemented quickly and structured so that its effects on aggregate spending are felt as much as possible within the next twelve months or so. Stimulus that comes too late will not help support economic activity in the near term, and it could be actively destabilizing if it comes at a time when growth is already improving. Thus, fiscal measures that involve long lead times or result in additional economic activity only over a protracted period, whatever their intrinsic merits might be, will not provide stimulus when it is most needed. Any fiscal package should also be efficient, in the sense of maximizing the amount of near-term stimulus per dollar of increased federal expenditure or lost revenue. Finally, any program should be explicitly temporary, both to avoid unwanted stimulus beyond the near-term horizon and, importantly, to preclude an increase in the federal government's structural budget deficit. As I have discussed on other occasions, the nation faces daunting long-run budget challenges associated with an aging population, rising health-care costs, and other factors. A fiscal program that increased the structural budget deficit would only make confronting those challenges more difficult.

Thank you. I would be pleased to take your questions.

References

Blinder, S. Alan, "Central Banking in Theory and Practice," MIT Press, 1998.

Bernanke, Ben S., "Testimony before the Committee on the Budget, U.S. House of Representatives, January 17, 2008.

Carmack, Patrick S.J., "The Money Masters" DVD, 2007.

Friedman, Milton and Schwartz, Anna Jacobson, "A Monetary History of the United States 1867 – 1960, Princeton University Press, 1993.

Ingham, Geoffrey, "The Nature of Money," Polity Press, 2004.

Keynes, John Maynard, "The General Theory of Employment, Interest and Money," First Harbinger Edition, 1964.

Marx, Karl, "Capital," www.marxists.org/archive.

Marx, Karl, "Critique of the Gotha Program," www.marxists.org/archive.

Podolski, T. M., "Socialist Banking and Monetary Control," Cambridge University Press, 1973.

Poole, William, "Money and the Economy: A Monetarist View," 1978

Rothbard, Murray N., "America's Great Depression," Fifth Edition, The Ludwig von Misses Institute.

Trotsky, Leon, "The Revolution Betrayed," www.marxists.org/archive.

Weintraub, Sidney, "Capitalism's Inflation and Unemployment Crisis," Addison Wesley Publishing Company, Inc, 1978.